The Cross and the Academy

Occasional Papers and Addresses

1975-2009

Dr. Paul J. Dovre

Lutheran University Press
Minneapolis, Minnesota

The Cross and the Academy

Occasional Papers and Addresses, 1975-2009
Dr. Paul J. Dovre, president emeritus

Prepared by The Dovre Center for Faith and Learning
Concordia College, Moorhead, Minnesota
Ernest Simmon, editor

Library of Congress Cataloging-in-Publication Data

Dovre, Paul John, 1935-
  The cross and the academy : occasional papers and addresses, 1975-
2009 / Paul J. Dovre.
      p. cm.
  Includes bibliographical references and index.
  ISBN-13: 978-1-932688-59-7 (alk. paper)
  ISBN-10: 1-932688-59-5 (alk. paper)
  1. Lutheran universities and colleges—United States. I. Title.
  LC574.D68 2011
  378.071'4173—dc22
                                        2011009911

Lutheran University Press, PO Box 390759, Minneapolis, MN 55439
www.lutheranupress.org
Manufactured in the United States of America

Table of Contents

Preface

This collection of addresses and papers begins with my inaugural in 1975 and concludes with recent reflections on Lutheran higher education. Most of these papers were presented in off-campus venues, at meetings of the Lutheran Education Conference of North American, at academic conferences, and in response to invitations from other colleges. One chapter was prepared and published at an on-line site sponsored by the Lilly Endowment. A smaller number of the papers were presented on the Concordia College campus in Moorhead, Minnesota, where I served as faculty member, dean, and president for thirty-eight years.

The title of this collection, *The Cross and the Academy,* reflects the common thread running through these materials—the relationship between faith and learning. This subject has been the principal professional interest of mine as a career educator. Early mentors, Joseph Knutson and Carl Bailey, sparked my interest in these matters and, as I became academic dean and later president of the college, it was clear to me that sustaining and engaging the mission of the college was the heart and soul of my work. So, without design, I began an independent study of history, theology, and philosophy that would inform my leadership and would eventually form the structure of this volume.

Higher education, and religious higher education in particular, has undergone virtually seismic change in the past fifty years—years that I experienced as a student, then as a faculty member, dean, president, and later as a consultant, observer, and writer. One essay, *Lutheran Colleges: Past and Prologue,* provides an autobiographical perspective on these matters. I observed Lutheran colleges and universities as they shifted from somewhat parochial institutions closely tied to the church and strongly identified by their sectarian missions to colleges and universities of academic distinction with looser church ties and more secular character. In more recent years, I have had the pleasure of witnessing a renewal of commitment to religious identity and mission in several Lutheran colleges.

These essays reflect my own responses to the evolving issues of my years in the Lutheran academy. Readers will note changes in the ways I expressed core convictions and responses to critical issues over time. I like to believe that these changes reflect my own growth and the evolution in the cultural and academic contexts in which I served.

Thanks are extended to many colleagues who shaped my thinking. On the other hand, none of those colleagues is responsible for what I have written here. The lists of publications following many of the essays identify writers whose work was especially helpful and inspiring to me over the years. I am grateful to each of them. Sheldon Green of the Concordia Communications office provided early and competent editorial assistance and my wife, Mardeth, was generous with both her encouragement and proofreading skills. Finally, a word of special gratitude is given to Ernest Simmons for both the sponsorship of this collection and the visionary leadership of the Dovre Center.

Paul J. Dovre

Introduction

The Lutheran tradition began in a university setting and at its heart has always had the dialectical interaction of faith and learning. This collection of occasional papers and addresses by Dr. Paul J. Dovre is an expression of that relationship in an over-fifty-year engagement with Lutheran higher education. Beginning first in 1952 as a student at Concordia College and continuing later as faculty member, dean, president, and currently interim president, Dovre has been in the midst of the Lutheran academic enterprise in the United States during some of the most interesting, challenging, and reforming times in its history. These essays reflect that transformation as educational institutions moved from mostly ethnic enclaves to major contributors to American higher education. As such they contain historical, cultural, theological, and educational insights which reflect the challenges faced by American culture and its educational systems as they moved from post-World War II into the twenty-first century, from modernism to postmodernism. In Lutheran higher education, few persons have had the privilege of serving in a major leadership role as long as Paul J. Dovre, and fewer still have done it in such a self-consciously reflective and insightful way that can be shared with others. This introduction will briefly highlight some of the recurrent themes that occur within this material and may assist the reader in making the most constructive use of these interesting essays.

The first theme is the **practical**, that is, the real necessity of balancing budgets, relating to constuencies, grappling with economic fluctuations, maintaining faculty quality and identity, and managing student recruitment and liberal arts curriculum reform. When one reads the inaugural address, "Look to the Rock" from 1975, it is almost as if it could have been written yesterday, for most of the issues considered are still with us today. Some of the contexts, both intellectual and cultural, do inevitably change, but these concerns are perennial and this first essay establishes the themes which flow through most of the subsequent essays, especially the role of relating the Christian faith to the life of the mind. One cannot help but be struck by both the consistency and insight that Dovre displays on these themes through the succeeding years.

The second theme is **historical,** where the richness and diversity of the Lutheran tradition in higher education is addressed. Most notably in the chapter "Lutheran Higher Education: A Heritage Revisited," Dovre summarizes the volume *Lutheran Higher Education in North America* by Richard Solberg clearly and concisely. In this essay, the reader is exposed to the ethnic heritage and cultural concerns that gave rise to Lutheran colleges and universities. It also addresses how theological disputes on such morally charged issues as predestination and slavery occasionally gave rise to competing institutions with alternative positions. In "Lutheran Higher Education in a Postmodern, Post-Christian Era," Dovre carries this historical and cultural analysis into our own day as the postmodern critique of modernist objectivism allows for a creative reemergence of religious thought in the academy, but not without consequence. As Dovre observes, "The confluence of modernist and postmodernist streams of intellectual construction has created an academic whirlpool. Christian apologists seeking a credible role in the academy may choose from among several options and must, therefore, contend with many competing constructions of reality." While religious perspectives can now be openly considered in academic reflection, they must be able to articulate themselves clearly and reasonably in a highly pluralistic context. Lutheran higher education is not immune to this shifting intellectual context and now must engage it in as serious a fashion as the previously more hostile secular and objectivist one. It is here that the Lutheran theological heritage can provide a great deal of support.

Third, **theological** themes are addressed drawing upon the richness of the Lutheran expression of the Christian tradition. The dialectical (interactional) relationship of Law and Gospel, saint and sinner, nature and grace, life before God and the world, faith and reason, Christian and academic freedom, the two kingdoms, vocation and community as well as the theology of the cross flow freely and frequently through these reflections. The foundational perspective is that the Christian, including the Christian scholar, is to live both in the world and mindful of a world to come. This understanding provides both a practical orientation of vocation for neighbor and a spiritual awareness of life created and sustained through the grace of God. These dialectics bring both freedom and reflection into academic life and provide not only a dynamic for Lutheran education but also a transcendent perspective from which to assess the human project in creation. Related to God through justifying grace and to the neighbor through loving service, the Christian intellectual is called to the pursuit of truth wherever it may lead as well as to the cultivation of justice and peace in the world. Lutheran higher education is one of the rare arenas in either church or society where the dual commitments to Christian freedom and academic freedom dialectically interact for mutual benefit. No questions are "off the table" for consideration, rather, all research and fields of thought are brought into interactive relationship with the life of faith. The Lutheran model of Christian higher education is one of dialectical interaction between faith and learning rather than of integration. The reader will find this model and the classical themes of the Lutheran theological tradition frequently in the essays of this volume, especially in "The Vocation of a Lutheran College–Revisited" and "A Lutheran Learning Paradigm."

The fourth theme is **educational,** where liberal arts education is central in articulating the purpose of Lutheran higher education. Modeled after the European, especially German, Latin school tradition, many Lutheran colleges began as academies which were preparatory schools for seminary and teaching. At the heart of this educational tradition, going back to the ancient Greek city-states, were preparation for citizenship and for the cultivation of one's own critical thinking and humanity. The "liberal" in "liberal arts" stands for freedom and the ability to think for oneself and to be able to discern meaning, beauty, justice, and truth independent of social or political mores. This was the good citizen to be cultivated in classical Western culture. Luther in his educational reforms, with the help of his colleague Philip Melanchthon, applied this pattern to all persons in society, not just to the social elite. The theological understanding of the priesthood of all believers opened the whole population to education and prompted one of the major social reforms of the sixteenth century. Public education is a direct social expression of the theological concept of justification by grace. This then leads Lutheran institutions to emphasize all of the liberal arts. This rich liberal arts legacy is addressed in many of the essays, especially "Lutheran Higher Education: A Heritage Revisited," and the diversity of responses and issues is developed in summarizing the work of Lilly Endowment funded initiatives in "Re-Examination and Renaissance: Lilly Sponsored Studies at the Turn of the Century."

Lastly, there is a **missional** theme, reminding readers that Lutheran higher educational institutions must keep a clear mission perspective which respects and reflects both their Christian and academic heritages as they strive to serve a constantly changing society. This theme is front and center in several chapters, especially "Through a Glass Darkly," "Mission in the Twenty-first Century," "Lutheran Intellectuals and the Church," and "The Lutheran Calling in Education." Coming out of the former American Lutheran Church, Dovre understands that colleges of the church are the church in mission in higher education. These institutions were products of mission and created for educational mission to the wider society as well as the church. This relationship, however, is never a static one. Major challenges to mission during the period of these essays come from the changing nature of education, the church, and the wider society in which they reside. In relation to society, colleges and universities needed to develop new programs and venues to address cultural, intellectual, economic, and technological change. In relation to the church, they have had to deal with schism (Lutheran Church–Missouri Synod) and merger (Evangelical Lutheran Church in America), as well as financial and structural reorganization. Maintaining continuity of mission in a relevant and appropriate way to both the wider society and the church during these times has required sustained clarity of purpose and commitment as well as flexibility in expression and implementation. Under President Dovre's leadership, Concordia College has navigated these changing intellectual currents and social and ecclesiastical whirlpools effectively, and his thought on these missional matters has become a resource for many sister institutions in the tradition as well.

Finally, Paul J. Dovre's rhetorical training and skill is amply apparent throughout this volume, no place more evidently than in the two sermon examples, "Our Father's World" and "To Sacred Truth." While a whole book is devoted to his sermons, *Holy Restlessness: Reflections on Faith and Learning* (Augsburg Fortress, 2009), it is appropriate that a glimpse of this style of writing is also included in this volume. Trained in classical rhetoric, Dovre is aware of the Aristotelian persuasive distinctions among *ethos*, *logos*, and *pathos*. *Ethos* is the power of one's personality, character, and reputation. *Logos* has to do with argument and evidence, with logic. And *pathos* appeals to our wants, desires, and emotions, through such things as our ideals, values, aspirations, and dreams. Dovre uses these distinctions to parse out the changes in Lutheran higher education in the last chapter of this volume (see "Lutheran Colleges: Past and Prologue"), but there is a sense in which these classical categories could also be used to describe the nature of the remaining contributions as well. One certainly gets a sense of the effective use of *pathos* in both the sermons and in many of the discussions on identity and mission. *Logos* is exercised not only in the thoughtful application of theological concepts to the educational context but also in the effective critique of culture and the intellectual streams that have flowed through the academy in the last fifty years. Finally, however, it is Paul J. Dovre's *ethos* which is most apparent here, for his personal character and reputation long precede the publication of this volume. The senior administrative statesman of Lutheran higher education in the ELCA, Dovre is a person whose wealth of experience and knowledge is frequently consulted by current deans, provosts, and presidents. It is fitting, then, that the first major publication of The Dovre Center for Faith and Learning be devoted to the work and reflection of one of the persons in whose names and honor the center was founded. This volume reflects the thought and life of a Lutheran Christian scholar, teacher, administrator, and churchman who has attempted to exercise his life and thought *Soli Deo Gloria*.

Ernest Simmons, Professor of Religion
Director, The Dovre Center for Faith and Learning

CHAPTER ONE

Look to the Rock

The 1975 Inaugural Address
Text: Isaiah 51:1-2

In an earlier era, inaugural addresses were thought of as a kind of credo statement of the incoming president's values and convictions, a sort of "Here I stand" oration. And, oh, yes, it was also acceptable to speak for longer than twenty minutes. This address met both of those criteria. It was a statement of my credo and it was longer than twenty minutes. The assembly of 2,000 friends, students, and visiting academics was patient and attentive—or so it seemed to me.

In the mid-1970s, the academy was still reeling from the social maelstrom of the 1960s. There had been many changes on campuses like Concordia's—changes in academic programs, in student lifestyle, in governance, in constituency relationships, and a lot more. I had experienced those changes and been in the midst of most of the struggles, some of which remained unresolved as I accepted the presidency of the college. So I took it as my challenge in this address to declare how I understood both our challenges and our resources. I presented and appealed to traditional arguments and proofs including the liberal arts, the theological and biblical foundation of the school, and the strong tradition of community. The Gospel call to reconciliation was at the heart of my early leadership as I sought to address both a constituency and a college that remained somewhat unsettled by the dynamics of the 1960s.

As the text for today, I turn to Isaiah 51:1-2: "Hearken to me, you who pursue deliverance, you who seek the Lord; look to the rock from which you were hewn, and to the quarry from which you were digged. Look to Abraham your father and to Sarah who bore you; for when he was but one I called him, and blessed him and made him many."

The writer of Isaiah addressed these words to a group of political exiles who were seeking deliverance and righteousness. He exhorted them to look to the rock of ages, that is to Abraham, the father of the faithful. Abraham had been one, but had been loved by God and made many. Concordia is not in exile, but we seek God's blessing and direction, and so I invite you to consider with me the basic dimensions of the rock from which Concordia College was hewn.

College presidents come and go, and the significance of their going turns mainly on the transcendent qualities of the colleges they lead. The contemporary vocabulary of higher education trades on words such as relevance, accountability, and secularization, and on the dilemmas posed by inflation, uncertain enrollments, government support and control. These words and issues may be different in three years and surely will be in ten. While we will all be accountable for our stewardship in dealing with these matters, I deem it important to reflect upon those resources and principles that have guided and shaped this college. We are not called to relive our past or to be a static and unchanging college—but in reflecting upon the rock from which we were hewn, we find reliable guideposts for dealing with the issues and opportunities before us.

The fundamental dimension of the rock from which Concordia was hewn is the Gospel of Christ—the Christ who called us to forgiveness and assured us of his love, the Christ who called us to a ministry of reconciliation and assured us of his eternal presence.

The pastors and farmers who established this college may have had some heated arguments about whether the college should be located in Crookston, Grand Forks, or Fargo-Moorhead and certainly the faculty disagreed about the content of the academic program. There was a good deal of political activity on both of these issues. But there were no arguments about the college's underlying purpose: "Concordia shall provide education and training for Christian service and leadership," they said. So, men and women called by the Gospel literally loved a college into being. In keeping with the Gospel, our pioneer founders were bold. They borrowed and raised money against good advice, they built buildings for more students than they enrolled, they beat the odds and survived economic depression, and they began talking about building an endowment in the early 1900s when such talk was more a measure of their faith than their capabilities. Yes, these were people made bold by the Gospel. By God's grace they could dare and they did, they could fail and they did, but through it all, God gave the college an increase. A measure of both their pride and competitive spirit was best expressed by one of the founding fathers who said, "These people are preparing to open Concordia College in Moorhead. These people are going to do a work for Christ and his church for which even the sons of New England will yet rise up and call them blessed."

The Gospel that inspired and emboldened the founders of Concordia still calls and enables us. Because of the Gospel, Paul's words to the Corinthians are fresh today: "Such is the confidence we have through Christ toward God. Not that we are sufficient of ourselves to claim anything as coming from us; our sufficiency is from God, who has qualified us to be members of a new covenant, not in a written code but in the spirit; the written code kills, but the spirit gives life" (2 Corinthians 3:4-6). In our contemporary rhetoric we speak of influencing the affairs of the world by sending into society thoughtful and informed men and women dedicated to the Christian life. It is a statement fully in keeping with the commitments of our founders, and it is a statement made possible by God's continuing work among us.

On the rock of the Gospel we are enabled to undertake the risks and excitement of this ministry at Concordia. From my mentors I have learned the meaning of faith in its institutional dimensions. It does not mean acting heedlessly, but it does mean acting in hope and confidence. The Gospel is sufficient for all seasons—seasons of drought and plenty, seasons of economic setback or public doubt, seasons of expansion or cutback, seasons of secularity or religious awakening. We know not what the next year or decade will hold, but we do know about Christ's faithfulness. It is on this rock that we sing the words of our college hymn, *Soli Deo Gloria*—to God alone the glory.

As we look to the rock, another of its dimensions is theology. In theology we work out our understanding of the Gospel and its application to our human context. When the founders of Concordia said that Concordia would "provide education and training . . . in conformity with the faith, confessions, and practices" of their synod, they were identifying the theological dimension of the rock from which Concordia was hewn.

There are some things that we Lutherans hold to be true about God, man, the world, and the relationship among them. Luther emphasized that God deals with us from the perspective of grace, and that is a revolutionary concept in any age. It was Luther's view that man is both justified by grace and is also a sinner, so we need to take sin seriously. He emphasized that the world was not a place to escape, but a realm of God's activity in which we are all called to address questions regarding the meaning and purpose of life, questions of human good, and issues related to faith and life. In short, it is a resource of central value to those engaged in the ministry of teaching and learning. It is a resource of special importance to the questions of this particular time.

For example, our technological prowess has created some disjunctions between what we know and what we do. Theologian Richard Salzmann says that we have lately tended to reduce reality to the pattern of our minds and thus ignore the laws of nature and supernatural issues. But God in Christ provides a basis for synthesis between Creator and creation, between knowledge and action, between neighbor and self. He makes new creatures of us and reconciles us to himself and then enables us to be agents of reconciliation in the world.

Consider one of the dominant themes in recent social commentary—the search for dependable values and a legitimate style of life. The new president of the American Psychological Association recently chided his fellow psychologists for siding with self-gratification over self-restraint. Allen Pifer of the Carnegie Corporation expresses concern for colleges and universities in dealing with moral issues, and his is one voice in a chorus of leading educators speaking to this issue. Perhaps the sense of moral drift is best dramatized by the title of Karl Menninger's recent book, *Whatever Became of Sin?* Those familiar with Luther's *Bondage of the Will* are acquainted with most of the arguments that are being rediscovered these days. For Lutherans, there is a group of propositions that speak to the limits of secular knowledge and human will and the need for self-discipline and restraint in the sanctified life. Seen in the light of the Gospel, these propositions become means of fulfillment rather than self-denial, means of seeing our neighbor and the requirements of justice and mercy with new clarity and power. Lutheran colleges have something distinctive to contribute to the dialogue about the human good when such questions are in style, as they are becoming today, and when they are not, as has been the case in recent times.

Then there are the questions of vocation that preoccupy so many of our young people today, questions that can be informed by what Luther had to say about the priesthood of all believers and the universal call to discipleship, a call that includes chambermaids and gardeners, surgeons and lawyers, businessmen and yes, pastors too.

I believe our colleges are called to be Lutheran, to bring to bear on the great questions of life and meaning the resources of our doctrines and tradition. To say we have the answers to all questions is to deny the search for truth for which Christ himself stood. And to say that we have something special to offer from a theological perspective is not to compromise our academic commitments. We have something important to contribute to our brothers and sisters of all faiths. We can make our contribution in a manner that safeguards the freedom and integrity of the academic enterprise. Lutheran theology is a dimension of the rock on which we were built. I believe that in taking seriously our theology, we may strike new fires in keeping with our historic mission. Let us claim this uniqueness, equip ourselves with it, and exercise it with joy and energy.

A third dimension of the rock on which Concordia was built is the commitment to quality liberal arts education. The commitment to good education was a matter of faith to the college's founders who must have been imbued by the spirit Luther reflected in saying, "If we wish to have excellent and apt persons for both civil and ecclesiastical government, we must spare no diligence, time, or cost in teaching and educating our children, that they may serve God and the world. . . ." This tradition of commitment to study in a religious setting goes back to Old Testament times, and Christ, in revealing himself, made himself knowable; thus the study of his life and revelation has been a dimension of education since the early church. In view of these traditions, it is no wonder that the founders of Concordia had a deep commitment to quality education, and it is appropriate for us to renew our commitment today. We are called to be a good college—called to excellence, if you will, a word that lost its currency some years back through misuse. Several years ago, Dr. Alvin H. Rogness, then president of Luther Seminary, said he expected our colleges to be excellent academic institutions. "Excellence in and by itself is a part of our witness to the Lord," he said. So it is today; we are called to develop our abilities to the maximum and to expect of our students the very best of which they are capable. The canons of academic excellence are the same at Concordia as at any secular institution—good scholarship and passion for the truth wherever it may be found.

In the early days of this college, there was a good deal of debate about the kind of educational program that the college should provide. Short courses in music, business, English, and the applied arts were the college's stock and trade until the early 1900s when a decision was made to develop a four-year baccalaureate level liberal arts program. It was nearly fifteen years from the date of that commitment to the awarding of the first baccalaureate degrees in 1917, but the issue was settled then—that Concordia should prepare students for Christian leadership and the liberal arts were the best means to that end.

Liberal arts education is based on the study of the most significant of man's traditions and the disciplines fundamental to understanding our world and ourselves. I appreciated Roger Goldwin's recent description of the value of liberal education: "We find we can develop very special skills that imitate the Creator himself, for we too can make new worlds, not out of nothing—but out of nothing more than a pencil, a straightedge, and a mind. Such skills . . . are called liberal because they free us from the restraint of our material existence and let us soar as free men and women in the realm of the mind." Through years of challenge from technology, unemployment, and vocationalism, we have remained in that tradition. Liberal arts education has been durable both because of the qualities it develops and its evolution. Innovation in content and method has transformed our program from time to time, giving it new vitality and currency. Our graduates have made distinguished records in the professions and in a range of careers including education, technology, agriculture, finance, and government.

As one looks to the present and future, the challenges confronting liberal arts education are rather immediate. We have agreed that diversity exists in higher education and that it is a good thing. After a decade of homogenization, it has also been agreed that uniqueness among individual institutions is a positive value. But in view of the challenges from a specialty-prone, job-minded and pragmatically oriented culture, we need to give definition to the value of liberal arts education. As Stephen R. Graubard remarked in assessing the future of higher education, "The liberal arts curriculum of yesterday would seem no longer to be adequate; there are few who detect very great vigor in what passes for 'general education' today. The issue of learning, its content and form, is recognized to be as important as any now confronting higher education." Graubard contends that what is at stake today is "the continued viability of the concept of a liberally educated person."

Indeed, what is useful to teach and know? How shall we achieve the liberating skills and understandings essential to the late twentieth century? Can we break down the walls of our disciplinary commitments? Can we resolve the confusion of voices on the issues of academic standards and goals?

I believe we should address these issues and, being somewhat traditional in our notions about liberal arts education, our resources for this inquiry are close at hand. But I believe such an examination can and should take place at each liberal arts college and there is some urgency about it, for the challenges are immediate and our claims are more philosophical than those of other sectors of education. Our claims are also conceived of as being less provable in a society prone toward pragmatic judgment. Therefore, at a minimum, we must reconsider and reaffirm what it is we are about and then state our claims far and wide with eloquence and persistence.

Look to the rock from which you were hewn in all of its dimensions—the Gospel, theology, the program, and, finally, a nurturing community. The nurturing community that is Concordia is made up of the constituents who have surrounded this college with their prayers and acts, the faculty and staff called to the ministry of teaching and leadership, and the students through whom the mission of the college is fulfilled. In his inaugural address in 1925, Dr. J. N. Brown summed it up for us when he said, "There are no pages in the history of our Lutheran church in America so thrilling in interest, so filled with self-sacrifice, so far reaching in permanent results as those pages recording educational activities of those far-sighted, freedom-loving, God-fearing Lutheran pioneers." The pages of Concordia's history bear out Dr. Brown's statement. Names like Guberding, Ness, Dosland, and Christanson abound in the chronicles of this college. Down through the decades the roll of saints includes scores of people from across these Great Plains and woodlands who saw a need and responded. While the founding fathers may not have succeeded in building a large vested capital endowment for Concordia, their example has given us a living endowment of congregations and church people, alumni and parents. Small wonder that Dr. Joseph Knutson at his inaugural in 1951 could say with confidence, "I know that my God and his people will not fail to uphold Concordia, her teachers and students, with their prayers and gifts."

Another group of this community's citizens are those privileged to teach and work here. Grose, Bogstad, Rognlie, Wollan, Fjelstad, and Ylvisaker are among the men and women who gave definition to the word commitment. They and their colleagues shaped our traditions of scholarship and study and offered models for the intellectual and personal lifestyle of generations of Concordia students. In our documents we say that the faculty and staff make more difference for good or ill than any other element in our college. That statement defines our challenge today as it has in the years gone by. Ours is a position of privilege, a position of almost unlimited possibilities for growth and ministry in Christ's church.

The other citizens of this nurturing community are the students. Their response to our teaching and leadership is what the college is all about. And again, the reputation that Concordia students have built is noteworthy. They have brought to the college great skill and good questions and have developed both to God's honor. With the help of those around them, they have gone on to distinguished careers both in this region and to the reaches of the earth.

The nurturing community that we call Concordia has always been more than the sum of its parts, and I think that is explained with the words Paul used in greeting the congregations at Philippi when he spoke of their "partnership in the Gospel from the first day until now" (Philippians 1:5). There has been a nurturing fellowship on the campus between the college, the constituency, and the church. The partnership has undergone change in composition and style. There were few among the early community who did not speak the mother tongue of Norway, whereas today we come from a wider variety of creeds and cultures. In much of our history the community style was more structured and formal than it is today.

Another reason for the tradition of nurture has been the strong sense of shared commitment that has been found among Concordia's members. The credit for the selection of the college's name is often given to the Rev. J. O. Hougen. He said, "Concordia is the goodness of harmony . . . (the) opposite of discord . . . (it) literally means hearts working together, hearts working in unison." This should not lead one to the erroneous conclusion that there have not been some battles here. Earlier I mentioned the faculty struggle over program content in our first decade, and I have been a participant in some great debates during the contemporary period. But the hearts have been working together, melded by the Gospel and the work of the Spirit among us, and disagreement and conflict have been possible here without fracturing the binding tie. The lesson is that we can continue to be a nurturing community by drawing on the resources of the Word and Sacraments. The music and worship traditions of Concordia are especially noteworthy, and few have passed through this campus without being influenced by them. With these resources we are free to express the new idea or critical insight that is often the key to new levels of service in education. These resources also enable us to provide an environment in which hearts are affirmed and nurtured by the Gospel.

This community will have special opportunities in the next several years. For example, many voices from the academy have been predicting that our institutions will suffer from atrophy in the "steady state," and their view is based on the assumption that the only source of institutional renewal is new personnel. But I would argue that a stable community built on secure and affirming relationships possesses the conditions for being a self-renewing community. Admittedly, that will not occur without some attention and energy, but I believe it is possible and the signs at hand are most hopeful.

Another opportunity that lies before the nurturing community relates to emerging levels of awareness and aspiration on the part of women and minority group citizens. We have passed the first blush of public concern when conscience-stricken legislators passed laws and funding bills designed to deal with an accretion of limiting self-concepts and institutional injustice. The funding levels have declined, and we have all become aware that the wheels of social change move slowly. But our call to justice and equal opportunity comes from the Gospel and not the social chic of a passing decade. As we provide a nurturing community for these special citizens, they become stronger and our college grows richer.

Look to the rock from which you were hewn in all of its dimensions: Gospel, theology, program, and nurturing community. Unlike the Israelites to whom our text was addressed, Concordia does not stand in political exile. But like the Israelites we seek direction for our future. We face the uncertainties of the future in the faith of our fathers. We affirm a future that holds new possibilities for reconciliation between and within disciplines and people and churches. We can make such an affirmation because the Gospel is fresh every morning, and it gives us both subject matter and grace for the task before us.

Paul Ricoeur said, "Hope is the same thing as remembering." In remembering the rock from which Concordia was hewn, we find our hope. I pledge myself to the rock from which Concordia was hewn, to the God and Creator of all things by whose grace this college is an agent of reconciliation. I make this pledge in joy and confidence, because God has promised to bless us with his love, his spirit, and his power. Amen.

CHAPTER TWO

What's Lutheran about Lutheran Colleges?

*This essay was published in **The Lutheran Standard** on February 3,*
*1976. The **Lutheran Standard** was the official publication of the Ameri-*
can Lutheran Church and reached a broad and diverse Lutheran audience.
I was in the early stages of my thinking about the distinctiveness of Lutheran
higher education. It was my view that a Lutheran college's distinctiveness
amounted to more than Lutheran head count, campus lifestyle, and some
courses in religion. The creeds, symbols, and traditions of the Lutheran Church
seemed to be a good place to center the discussion about distinctiveness.

What does it mean to be a Lutheran college? This question is not
asked for casual discussion. Its answers may determine whether the
schools of our church live or die. Our Lutheran church colleges have
traditionally defined themselves in terms of commitment to Christian
purpose. They have spoken of themselves as places which seek to express Christian community, endeavor to nurture a Christian lifestyle,
and attempt to carry forward the traditions and confessions of the
Christian faith through the academic study of religion. But more can
be said about the duties of our Lutheran church colleges.

Sydney Ahlstrom, a historian from Yale University, has pointed
out that the scholastic movement in the seventeenth century and the
critical movements of the nineteenth century were strongly influenced,
nearly dominated, by scholars with distinctively Christian interests
and traditions. Lutherans were especially evident in the critical movement. Their task was great, and their goal noble. They sought to
understand and interpret the world and Christianity through confrontation of the two. They did it in confidence that Christ stood for
truth and the scholar was free, indeed obliged, to follow that example.

Ahlstrom also has observed that it was the Lutherans—almost exclusively in Germany—who founded the principle of academic freedom. So we say that as Lutheran church colleges we have a special freedom to teach and learn. It is a freedom derived from Christ and a freedom which involves a responsibility for excellence in all things, including the claims we make. What does this imply? It means we can pursue any questions; there is no forbidden ground. We avoid oversimplification, false reasoning, and all the other byways of intellectual integrity and rigor.

What serves Christ and his church best is the truth as we find and test and transmit it. But seeking this truth is not a crusade that abandons care of human need or condones teaching which destroys growing or uncertain hearts.

Being a church college means a freedom to teach and learn from Christian ground. The Lutheran church is a confessional church. There are certain things we believe—things which may have a very favorable effect on learning and life at our colleges. For example, the first article of the Apostles' Creed acknowledges that it is God who has made us and all that is. He was and is creator. There may not be a "Christian" science or a "Christian" math, but the stance of faith makes a difference in how we understand matter, motion, and the symbolic representation of reality. Our faith may relate to what purpose we see for the universe. With this view of creation in mind, students are not simply names on an IBM card or on a list of pre-law or pre-medicine prospects. They are beings created by God with majesty and promise.

In the second article of the Apostles' Creed we acknowledge important truths about our nature and about the one who redeems us and our society. History for us is the sacred story of God's activity among people. Hence, for us, study in the humanities and the sciences may be informed by our doctrine of man and our understanding of the way God works through history. Our doctrines of creation, original sin, and sanctification provide points of definition regarding what is moral, what is good, what is acceptable, and what contributes to a holy life.

In the third article of the Creed we hear the call to community on earth, to fellowship with God through the Holy Spirit, and to eternal life. We acknowledge there is for us an end line, a sense of direction, and an assurance of comfort—all of which have possible effect on where we see our subject matter leading us, on how we define the forces of change and continuity, and on how we relate to one another.

I like this statement from St. Olaf College's centennial publication, *Identity and Mission in a Changing Context:* "...the stance of faith may make a difference in the interpretation and use of knowledge. The Christian has, by faith, a picture of the way things are, how God and man and the world stand to each other, and what we have to do with each other."

Being a Lutheran church college involves the freedom and responsibility to confront culture. Jesus moved about in the culture of his day. He addressed it directly, and he spoke in parables about it and about his Father's wishes for it. Jesus did not try to set up a protected, small group in a town or on a campus. Instead, he moved out and spoke to people in their situations. He set an example of dialogue with culture. What the obligation to nurture dialogue between Christ and culture implies is not simple. Augustine, Luther, Kierkegaard, and Niebuhr are among those who have considered the matter. The dialog is lively and, at its best, open and engaging. It fosters disagreements and is hopefully a service to the church.

For a church college, the work of relating faith to questions of theology, politics, science, art, history, and human behavior is the essence of that dialog. And we are free to do that! The outcome of this dialog is sometimes joy and peace, other times conflict and instability—but then Jesus both ran the money changers out of the temple and fed the hungry in the wilderness.

Being a Lutheran church college involves the celebration of Word and Sacrament. Dr. Gordon Lathrop, former campus pastor at Pacific Lutheran University and now on the faculty of Wartburg Seminary, has said that the uniqueness of a Lutheran college is that "it is a place where the celebration of the Word and Sacraments is fostered; the Christian symbols are held up explicitly and proclaimed, so that the confrontation between Word and world can in fact take place."

If we are to teach and learn and lead from Christian ground, if we are to exercise our freedom in Christ in responsible ways, and if we are to have a quality dialogue between faith and culture, then the Word must be preached and the Sacraments must be celebrated, for by these practices, in all their mystery, our faith gains its strength and finds its nurture. In the absence of the Word and the Sacraments, we risk separating our faith from knowledge, life from learning, Christ from culture.

Sometimes the celebration of Word and Sacrament may seem more discipline than delight. But the experience of worship is not a fringe activity for a Lutheran church college. Worship is absolutely essential, and it is no accident that chapel services and even student congregations have been common at our church colleges.

To live and teach and learn at a Lutheran church college means being committed to Christian purpose, striving to express Christian community, seeking to nurture and demonstrate a Christian lifestyle, fostering the academic study of religion, encouraging the search for truth, and engaging in a vigorous dialogue between faith and the world. In taking seriously the theology and traditions which shape our Lutheran colleges, we may strike new fires in keeping with our historic purposes. Thus we will continue to be Lutheran colleges of the church.

Reprinted from *The Lutheran Standard* with permission of *The Lutheran*.

CHAPTER THREE

Our Father's World

Homily Delivered at Homecoming Service of Celebration
October 5, 1980
Text: Genesis 1:26-31

This homily was presented at the annual homecoming service on the occasion of the dedication of the Jones Science Center. This was a facility for which we had waited a long, long time and, because of its multimillion dollar cost—an amount of money the college had never raised before—it had been an especially challenging endeavor. So the dedication of this building was a cause for great celebration among both the alumni gathered at homecoming and the students and faculty for whom this new facility would prove so useful. My purpose in this homily was to celebrate the event by placing the study of science into the theological context of our mission and the social context of our time. I included a discussion of the relationship between science and religion, a subject that, at the time, was not very controversial. Who would have imagined that, by the end of the century, it would be revisited with such energy and passion?

If a stranger came into our midst today and observed here the readers and the readings, the liturgy and the banners, the choirs and the singing of God's people, he might logically ask, "What's this all about? What's all the commotion?" Well, we would answer, we have come here to dedicate a building. It is not just any building, of course. It is a building devoted to the study of the earth and its inhabitants, the rocks and the plants, the animals and the people, the fish and the birds, the reptiles and the insects. It is the world the Psalmist spoke about as being full of beauty and wonder.

But the stranger in our midst would say, "There must be something special about this building and about what will be studied here."

That is true, for us there is something special about it—for the study of life and the world is not some disconnected, isolated, esoteric discipline, because this is our Father's world! In the first article of our Creed, we express our belief that God created it. Indeed, we Lutherans have always been a first article church, affirming the beauty and the joy of the created order. We are a culture-affirming church. So for us, to discover the truth about our Father's world is a calling, in and of itself.

This is our Father's world. But the stranger in our midst would say, "What do you mean by such talk?" It does not mean that we, as believers in the Father, know how it was all done, but we do claim to know who did it. The church has always been in trouble when it has tried to take over science, whether we go back to the period centuries ago when well-intentioned Christians tried to write the theories of Copernicus and Galileo out of the church or to the modern time when some claim a narrow answer, sacred or secular, to the "how" question. How the world began is an important question, and we address ourselves to it with rigor in the study of science and human life. But the central question of Genesis 1 is not how it was done but whose world it is. And Genesis speaks to that question: It is God's world. As one commentator put it, "If this is not God's world, even the most frenzied arguments could not make it so. But if it is God's world, we do not need to be afraid of anything it actually reveals." On that we base, finally, our academic freedom to pursue the facts and to test all things, for in God's world we need not fear what is revealed about how the world was created. This, we believe, is the key to both right-minded science and sound theology. God created it; it is his world. That is an article of faith.

Another of the revelations of Genesis about God's world is that we have a special place in it. First of all, we have a special relationship to the Creator. In the book of Genesis, the plants and the animals are referred to in impersonal terms, but human beings are referred to by God in personal terms. Indeed, God spoke to Adam and Eve as "thou" and "you." Unique among all the elements of creation, we are designed to be in fellowship with God. The history of Israel, the life of Christ, and the ministry of Paul all underscore that promise. Relationship and family, parent and child, many members of one body with Christ as the head—our tradition is built on the images and reality of relationship. As Thomas Carlyle once put it to a group of scientists, "The mystery of man can be understood only if you put him into relation to Him who gives him his life, calls him by name." Luther put it similarly when he said that our dignity as human beings does not rest on our own human qualities, but rather upon the relationship with which God dignifies us. "He makes us His partner, He addresses us, He allows us to deal with Him" (Helmut Thielicke, *How the World Began*).

The second quality of human beings is that we were given special sovereignty. We are told in Genesis that after God created male and female, he blessed them and said, "Be fruitful and multiply, and fill the earth and subdue it; and have dominion over the fish of the sea and over the birds of the air and over every living thing that moves upon the earth." Broadman put it well when he said, "If a man is cold, he may light a fire; and if he is hot, he may build an air conditioner. Animals within the limits of their instincts must adjust to the environment; they cannot change it. Man can change it for better or for worse."

This sovereignty does not mean that we are to despoil the earth and make of it what we will. No, it's a delegated sovereignty, and therefore we stand in a position of responsibility. As Helmut Thielicke put it, "We are not to rule and subdue the earth because we stand above the other creatures, but only because we stand under God and are privileged to be his viceroys." The sciences of earth and humanity that will be pursued in this building are means by which we are privileged to exercise the sovereignty of God. So doctors will be trained to discover the orders of creation and push back the barriers of disease, and teachers will be prepared to understand people and communicate truth, and future servants in society will discover and embody the things which make for community.

We humans are special in that we stand in relationship to God and we have been given sovereignty. We are special in still a third way: We have been given a particular freedom. We have been given the freedom to choose between good and evil, between justice and injustice, between obedience and rebellion. While the other creatures of the world cannot fail to fulfill their destiny, human beings were given that capacity. We may find great joy, great fulfillment, or great tragedy according to our exercise of that freedom. We can understand our relationship, our dominion, and our freedom as gifts of God, giving us a special place in his world. They were given to us as blessings so that we would have the potential for joy, for fulfillment, and for fellowship with the Father. "For God saw everything that he had made, and behold, it was very good."

But the stranger in our midst, hearing the story I have told, might still say, "Well, things were great to start with, but what happened?" More particularly, he might charge that a funny thing happened on the way to the garden. Adam and Eve ate the forbidden fruit. These people with a special relationship to God, people with special sovereignty and freedom—they did the wrong thing after all! We Lutherans call it "the fall."

I think the first thing we want to recognize about the fall is that it was really quite a subtle thing. The devil was a wily person. He made an offer which seemed innocent: "Why don't you have this apple?" Indeed, why not? And isn't it so that our decisions often turn on subtle points? A voice within us says, "I'll show you a fascinating thing. I'll give you a comfortable place. Wouldn't you enjoy some prestige, some social acceptance? Why not have a little fun, and it won't even cost! After all, you deserve to be happy." There are lots of apples in the garden—sweet, delicious, and innocent enough. The temptor often comes to us in the guise of respectability, in the pursuit of happiness. Then, little decisions start adding up, and the statisticians read out the ugly toll on what happens on an average day in America: Six thousand couples wed and three thousand divorce, more than twenty-seven hundred children run away from home and an equal number of teenagers get pregnant, and over thirty-two hundred women have abortions.

After all, it should be our right in the pursuit of happiness to produce as much as we can so that we may eat as much as we like. That is also like picking an apple from a tree in an abundant orchard. Then a recent report on the future called "Global 2000" tells us that the world's population will increase fifty-five percent by the year 2000, the world's tillable soil will be menaced by erosion and the buildup of salt and alkali, and hundreds of millions of people will be hungry. By one estimate "between half a million and two million species—largely insects and plants—could be extinct by 2000, mainly because of air pollution and the loss of natural habitats." Because we have to protect ourselves, we and the Russians build armament upon armament. I mean, we want security and so it seems like picking an apple from a tree to build more missiles. But with each decision, we increase the chances of unintentional world holocaust. And, mind you, each of the decisions leading to these consequences is slow and subtle—kind of like deciding whether or not to take an apple from the garden.

But sin does not come only in the form of the subtle choosing of an apple. It also comes to us in the form of murder in the field, acts of calculation and volition. When Cain slew Abel it was an act of volition, a murder in the field. So it was when David slew the husband of Bathsheba. So, too, it was in Sodom and Gomorrah, cities well warned of their impending doom. The holocaust was no set of subtle decisions, but a grand design of evil, made by knowing and rational men. When millions of people are sent out of a South Asian country to become the innocent victims of starvation, it is indeed murder in the field. And even now, the suppression of freedom to the innocent millions in Namibia stands as an indictment of our brand of civilized conduct.

Adam and Eve were given the knowledge of good and evil and the freedom to choose between the two. It was part of their sovereignty; it was integral to their freedom. Cain and Abel had that choice, too, and all the rest down through the ages to us. Sometimes the choice was like choosing an apple from a tree in the garden and other times like committing murder in the field. This is our Father's world, but when you look at our record in this sophisticated and scientific age, you are pretty confident that God would say, "It is not good." And so, like Adam and Eve, we want to run and hide—whether we have been taking apples from the garden or committing murder in the field.

But in the face of all this, the most important truth of all is that the Father of our world continues to claim us. Indeed, his creative activity goes on. God did not wind up the world like a clock and go away to leave us to our own devices and his world to some inevitable catastrophe. No, God created us to be in relationship to him, and

God continues to create relationship. Because of their choices, Adam and Eve were forced out of the garden and made to labor, but they were not removed from God's presence. And Cain, who slew Abel—God did not send him to some ultimate fate. No, instead, God put his mark of protection and providence on him. David, who killed the husband of his lover and lamented over his enemies pains—God stayed in touch with David. He did not abandon Job, who felt put upon and tested. He would not let go of Paul, in spite of his persecution, or Peter, in spite of his denials. Each of these people and hundreds of others in the Bible chose to break relationship with God, but in each case, God reached out to recreate relationship. Then, God sent his Son to make the statement for all time and all peoples, and God sent his Spirit, who dwells with us still, restoring and renewing relationship.

This is the God who counts the hairs on our heads; you better believe he knows about our daily anxieties. This God, who cares about one lost sheep, you can be sure, knows about those starving in Uganda and seeking freedom in Namibia and South Africa. If a thousand years in God's sight is like a day, then he is the God of our history—yours, mine, and this college's. This is our Father's world, and he continues to create relationship with us. Yes, and he also renews the invitation to have dominion over the earth. Paul tells us that reconciliation, wholeness is the plan. In Christ, God renewed the call to have dominion over the earth by calling us to be his disciples, to feed his sheep, to look after the hungry and diseased, and to be God's ambassadors in reconciling the world to himself.

We are partners in the ongoing work of creation. That is the premise for this college, for the building we will dedicate, and for the teachers and students who will inhabit the place. Look at the history of the partnership in creation through the graduates of the departments we recognize today:

- A home economics graduate combines a career in university teaching with pioneering educational efforts in the underdeveloped nations of South America.
- A biology graduate attains international prominence in parasitology while pushing back the night of one of the largest groups of killer diseases in the world.

- Another graduate is in charge of providing food for university students in Tanzania.
- Another is recognized as the outstanding high school biology teacher in his state.
- Other alumni serve on the medical staff of the most prestigious clinic in the world.
- Yet others provide for the health needs in isolated rural areas, serving as both community leaders and health specialists.
- And there have been medical missionaries by the dozen and school and university teachers by the hundreds who come from this place—all involved in the continuing, creative activity of our Father's world.

The reconciling Christ invites us to claim our freedom in him. Just think what future generations of teachers and students of home economics and biology, claiming that freedom, can look forward to in the ongoing creation of our Father's world. Because of enlightened investment and development policies, innovations in agriculture, population control and health improvement, the per capita income in the poorest nations of the world nearly doubled in the past twenty-five years and life expectancy has increased by nearly twenty percent. The scientists of today may want to join in this creative activity. We are told that DNA will offer the possibility of new approaches to the treatment of cancer, that a new breed of fish is being developed which may provide a rich protein resource for developing nations, and that a new legume may provide another food source for these same people. Our scientists, our teachers, and doctors can be part of that reconciling activity because we are rooted in the land and therefore we have the opportunity to bring a fresh theology for man and his use of the earth.

God saw everything he had made and, behold, it was very good! Not the sins of Adam and Eve, or David and Paul, or Hitler and the Viet Cong, or you and me—none of that can separate us from the re-creating love of God. Surely, we have experienced the creative work of God in our lives, in this place, among our people. In that sure and certain hope, we dedicate a place of study to be part of God's continuing creation. In that sure and certain hope, we, the citizens of God's world, can sing a new song. Amen.

CHAPTER FOUR

To Sacred Truth

1984 Homecoming Worship
Texts: John 8:31-36 and 2 Timothy 1:3-14

I have preached a number of homilies at the college's annual homecoming worship service. This one addresses the relationship between secular truth and sacred truth, two staples of conversation in the Lutheran church and its academies.

College hymns and songs are familiar to us. Yesterday at the football game we sang our fight song, remembering the familiar words: "Stand up and cheer, stand up and cheer for old Concordia." That song has served us well through the years, win or lose.

College hymns are another matter. There are thousands of them. Almost every college has one. But usually they are paraded out on rare occasions and sung with restraint and close attention to the script. Concordia's hymn is different than that. For one thing, we sing it often—at years' beginning, at year's end, and several times in between. An alumni meeting is never complete until our anthem has been sung. We sing it often because it is singable and it says something. "On firm foundation"—what strength those words convey! "With love and hope surrounded" expresses the spirit of the place. "In strength and faith forever" is a statement of purpose and direction. And if you are a regular homecoming participant you have heard, in recent years, sermons on each of those themes.

There is one more phrase that begs our attention: "To sacred truth, Concordia, may thou 'er faithful be." Now there is a package for you, for me, for us—and it is that package that I want to unpack with you this morning. Literally hundreds of colleges say that they are committed to the search for truth. But not many are presumptuous enough to quest after sacred truth. I am going to suggest that there are two kinds of truth, secular and sacred. Colleges sometimes confuse them. But it is our call, as a college of the church, to pursue both kinds of truth and, indeed, to shape the one with the other.

Secular truth is the truth we seek and know about the world. Let me recall some important secular truths: The earth is round, and water consists of two parts of hydrogen and one part of oxygen. Those are secular truths which are important to us. So, too, is the statement that every minute of every day $1.3 million is spent for military purposes while, in that same minute, thirty children in poor countries die, mostly from starvation and malnutrition. In those countries there are few resources to stimulate increased food production or better health care. Such truths are important to us. We need to know them, and we seek to know other secular truths like what causes inflation, or how to lower the federal deficit, how to find new ways of growing tremendous amounts of food to feed the people in poor countries, and how to ease the social and political evolution of developing nations in ways that will secure both justice and peace.

The search for secular truth is part of the agenda of this college. There is theological rootage for that going all the way back to God's injunction in Genesis that we should subdue the earth and have dominion over it. Mind you, that was not a call to exploitation, but to stewardship. We Lutherans are a first article church. We affirm the joy and beauty of the earth. Like our spiritual ancestor Martin Luther, we affirm the world and consider the discovery of secular truth about it to be a calling in and of itself. In the "Agenda for Concordia's Academic Life" completed earlier this year, our faculty senate affirmed that we are called to exercise stewardship of our intellectual potentialities—to be excellent inquirers in order that we and our students may be contributing members of society, what Luther identified as "able, learned, wise, honorable, and well-educated citizens."

If Concordia is to be about the business of influencing the affairs of the world, of preparing well-educated citizens, then we had better be good at secular truth. You cannot feed hungry people with sympathy, nor can sick people be made well with good intentions. The young cannot learn without teachers to lead them, and the shackles of nuclear and political servitude will not be lifted without wise peacemakers. Yes, we must be wise about this world we would influence, so we need to acquire secular truth. Such truth may give us a sense of liberty, it can free us from superstitions, and it enables us to set goals and provides us with the tools to achieve them.

Secular truth is on this college's agenda. That is why we gather first-rate faculty with experience in the search for such truth and we assist and support them in leading others in that quest. We have put in place buildings, necessary instruments and equipment, and books in order that we may carry out that agenda with quality—yes, with excellence. We are always amending and revising curricula in order to do this task still better. That is the tradition of this college from the early days when Rasmus Bogstad roamed the countryside in search of contributions to build Old Main to the days of Luther Jacobson, who will enroll four hundred C-400 members all by himself.

If that is the case for secular truth, what about the other side of it? What about sacred truth? In the Gospel today Jesus was engaged in dialogue with some people who were worldly wise; they surely knew their secular truth. Jesus said to them, "If you continue in my Word, you are truly my disciples, and you will know the truth, and the truth will make you free." A few years later, Paul was to tell Timothy: "Guard the truth that has been entrusted to you by the Holy Spirit." The truth they were talking about is that God became human in order to reconcile us to himself. He comes to free us all from bondage: "from death, sin and the power of the devil," as our confession reads. It is, wrote theologian Alvin Rogness, a truth which frees us from guilt, from the dominion of sin, and finally from death itself. Now there is truth for you. Summed up in three words: God loves you. That is the truth we call sacred.

Now this truth is not about better curricula, higher test scores, faster computers, better missiles, or even healthier bodies or better government. No, this truth has the power to make us free. It is not pie in the sky by and by; it is here and now truth. You see it in the eyes of a mother and father as they watch their child's first moments of life. You experience it when a college family is comforted in a time of tragedy. You hear it when the Word is preached in faithfulness. You taste it in the breaking of bread and the drinking of wine, his body and blood. You praise it when you watch our students gathering resources to build a school in Tanzania. You acknowledge it when the search for meaning takes precedence over the search for cash.

Sacred truth is what that durable dozen had in mind when they gathered in April of 1891 to establish this college. It is what I.F. Grose responded to when he agreed to become the first principal. So we see that Herman Monson and Borghild Torvik clearly knew what they were doing when they wrote the enduring lyrics of our hymn.

Well, it is a good message our hymn contains, this sacred truth idea. But I must hasten to demure in my preaching. For you will recall in the Gospel text, Jesus ran into some problems in Galilee and Jerusalem with his sacred truth. The folks in that land knew well their secular truth and, as long as Jesus healed the sick among them, fed the hungry, and held out political possibilities, they followed along. But when he spoke of sacred truth, about the bread of life as contrasted to the bread of wheat, then they were not so sure. This talk of truth and freedom they did not understand. We are descendants of Abraham, they said, and we are already free. The bondage of sin and the sacred truth of freedom was, to them, strange talk indeed. They couldn't see past their understanding of freedom—the food, the healing, and the political possibilities. Without knowing it, they were running the risk of gaining the world and losing their souls.

It is not an unfamiliar experience to twentieth-century types either, is it? Which of us does not structure lives around the secular truths of the Galileans? Better health, better food, and better jobs for better living is our unspoken motto. In this election year, surveys reveal that economic issues are central and humanitarian issues are peripheral for our electorate. The current education and reform movement in this nation which was heralded by the landmark study, "A Nation at Risk," is primarily motivated by a concern for secular truth—for finding it and transmitting it more effectively.

Surveys of college students find that they are putting their emphasis on "survival skills," and institutions of higher education respond to such impulses by developing increasingly specialized, technically-oriented curricula. These developments led Georgetown University's President Timothy Healy to say that we are far too preoccupied with what works rather than with what matters. The noted scholar James Billington blames the universities for failing to transmit values to students. This, he said, is especially serious, because historically universities have had the task of imparting ethics and tradition to the leaders of tomorrow.

Colleges of the church have not been immune to such tendencies, for they are, after all, human institutions reflecting society. Many colleges, once citadels of the quest for sacred truth, have sold out to the demands of secular survival. Their commitment to sacred truth is limited to the presence of a campus chaplain, a religion requirement in the curriculum, and the presence of some church body representatives on the governing board. But from there on the secular takes charge. The faculty is selected exclusively on the basis of such criteria and students, too. The selection of trustees is governed by secular influence. And the discussion of sacred truth is tuned to the expectations of a secular society—what will work and what will sell!

In the midst of all this stands our hymn, "To sacred truth, Concordia, may thou 'er faithful be." And Jesus' words, "Continue in my Word, and you shall know the truth." And Paul's words, "Guard the truth that has been entrusted to you." That word, that truth, is of salvation and reconciliation, of judgment and forgiveness, of counsel and amendment. It is different than the secular truth of better health for better living, of security from cradle to grave, and of being all that we can be. It defies the secular truth that we get what we pay for, that we are masters of our own destiny, and that what we feel is all that matters. Jesus points to the truth that matters most, and it is a lamp to guide us, a light for our path. He clears out the brambles, even in the valley of the shadow. Jesus takes us to mountaintops, places of health and joy where life is full of meaning. And he invites us to a community with the saints, fellow travelers upon whom he bestows his presence. To such truths you and I—and this college—are called to be faithful in two ways.

First, by proclaiming God's Word, his sacred truth. It is a fount of knowledge and grace for our journey. They say that one of the things most attractive to new Christians is the Bible because it is a source of dependable truth. Most of us take that for granted, but Jesus calls us to continue in his Word, and Paul told Timothy to guard that truth. So this college is called to proclaim that truth and continue in it. The impact of that truth upon the college is simply incredible. It has been a source of comfort in times of hardship, a source of courage in times of challenge, and a source of direction in times of opportunity. Continue in the Word, Concordia. Let this be central to the work of planners, the leadership of faculty, the studies of students, and the prayers of all. This Word, this sacred truth, is what distinguishes us as a college of the church. We depend on it. Without it we would be another college—good at secular truth but not distinguished by a cross. So let us proclaim that sacred truth, and place it at the center of our lives and our college.

Second, let us relate the sacred truth to the secular truth. Jesus did that. He ministered to people in context—the farmers and carpenters, the politicians and teachers. His parables and dialogues brought sacred truth to bear on secular life around him. Again, this is our Lutheran tradition. When Luther spoke of two kingdoms—the secular and the sacred—it was with the understanding that the sacred was to shape and guide the secular. That is what Concordia needs to be about. In Concordia's blueprint for the decade of the 1980s, our commitment was stated in these words: "We have a peculiar obligation as inquirers in a Christian community to pursue the implications of our Christian commitment for our disciplines and to pursue the implications of our disciplines for our Christian commitment." We mean to influence the affairs of the world in God's name. This world we would influence needs business people sensitive to ethical concerns, medical people who are tuned to all our health needs, scientists who are concerned about the use and discovery of knowledge, counselors who are expert in dealing with the fundamental questions of life, teachers who can address the "why" questions as well as the "how," and politically informed people who can bring the insights of their faith to bear on the public agenda.

It is our business to be informed about the world, so we pursue secular truth. It is an honorable and necessary Christian vocation. But we also have been entrusted with God's sacred truth. It is a truth that sets us free. It is a truth on which this college was established and on which our lives are built. To sacred truth may we ever faithful be. Amen.

CHAPTER FIVE

Lutheran Higher Education: A Heritage Revisited

Wartburg Seminary, April 21, 1987

In 1986 the Lutheran Educational Conference of North America completed preparation of a volume entitled **Lutheran Higher Education in North America,** *a history of Lutheran colleges and universities on North American soil. Its principal researcher and author was Richard Solberg. I chaired the planning and editorial committee for this project and it constitutes my principal resource for this lecture which – to put my credentials as accurately as possible – makes me a secondary or, at best, a tertiary source. This lecture was presented on the eve of the formation of the Evangelical Lutheran Church in America and in the latter part of the essay I articulate my analysis of the future of the relationship between the new church body and the colleges. This lecture was presented at a spring convocation at Wartburg Seminary.*

In the epilogue to the volume **Lutheran Higher Education in North America,** Richard Solberg wrote: "The most influential educational vehicle of (the Lutheran) tradition in North America has been the Lutheran college." I appreciate having the opportunity to revisit the heritage of Lutheran higher education with you today. I shall examine first the origins of these institutions, then assess their role and influence, and, finally, suggest some factors which may have a decisive influence on their future.

One of the most pithy descriptions of the history of Lutheran colleges was offered by a friend in this succinct statement: "Established by intention; located by accident; sustained by faith, hope, and charity." All over-simplifications run their hazards but, as such devices go, this one is not, as we shall see, far off the mark.

That is particularly true of the first thesis—that the colleges were established by intention: theological intention, social-political intention, and educational intention. But before we consider educational intentions on American soil, we must begin with the educational intentions of Lutheran reformers in Germany, because Lutheran higher education on this continent had its roots in the German university and the Reformation. The Reformation stirred educational reform by its affirmation that the Gospel should be central to the faith and available to all. Luther initially believed that religious education should be the responsibility of the family, but he came to see that that was unworkable. Schools, in turn, were in a deplorable state, so Luther and other Reformation leaders began to change things through reform and strengthening the so-called Latin or elementary schools. In a 1530 sermon, "On Keeping Children in School," Luther argued for the establishment of higher schools to supply pastors and provide civic leadership that would insure good and orderly government. As Solberg reports, these schools would follow a "humanistic approach to learning" in the conviction that "thorough intellectual preparation of professional leadership for church and community (was) fundamental to the broad intentions of the Reformation." Luther was committed to liberal arts education and argued specifically for the inclusion of the study of language, history, poetry, rhetoric, science, music, and even gymnastics. Melanchthon was to carry these ideas forward through the eventual establishment of the gymnasium and the reform of the universities.

This system of education including Latin schools, gymnasium, and university were primary transmitters of the Lutheran tradition in higher education. The system fed a stream of well-schooled young men through the system and the universities "became the creators and interpreters of the theological and intellectual currents which flowed through Europe for the next three centuries." In view of this history, it is easy to understand why Lutherans in America would turn to education for their leadership needs and their theological interests. And they would often turn to education of a particular kind, the broad-based, humanistic education which was characteristic of the liberal arts.

Theological intentions were easily the major influence in the establishment of most Lutheran colleges in America. That was true of the very oldest, Gettysburg Seminary. Established in 1826, the early professors found that their students were not well prepared, whereupon Gettysburg College was established in 1832. Gettysburg College's concern was for an educated ministry. And it would be like most of the early colleges in that it was really both seminary and college. Both were established in response to theological concerns growing out of the Great Awakening which had rocked the country and the Puritanism which held sway at that time. Samuel Smucker was founder of both the college and the seminary, and he was concerned to advance the countervailing character of Lutheran theology and practice. The German gymnasium was the model for the curriculum. The program was a combination of preparatory school and two to three years of college work. The curriculum included five years of Greek and Latin, four years of math through calculus, ancient and modern geography, philosophy, political economy, moral philosophy, English grammar, and rhetoric. The influence of Gettysburg College and Seminary was substantial. Its graduates were founders or first presidents of twelve Lutheran colleges, nine of which are still in existence: Wittenberg, Roanoke, Capital, Newberry, Thiel, Muhlenberg, Susquehanna, Carthage, and Midland Colleges.

The theological winds of the 1800s were blowing in many directions, and that accounted for the creation of the next two colleges in the sequence. Samuel Smucker had been educated at Princeton, and some of the theological influences of that institution led him and his colleagues to offer what they called a conditional affirmation of the Augsburg Confession. However, many Lutherans were moving toward a more conservative confessionalism in the wake of revivalism. Struggles emerged at Gettysburg Seminary and College and in the church at large between the so called "American Lutherans" who followed Smucker and the so-called "Old Lutherans" who took their stand on the unaltered Augsburg Confession.

The Ohio Synod took up the cause of the "Old Lutherans" and felt that they needed to establish their own seminary and college, both to meet the needs of German immigrants moving into Ohio and to address the theological crisis that stirred them. But not all the

Ohio Germans saw the issues the same way, so two colleges and seminaries and synods emerged. The Ohio Synod was meticulous about the use of German. The Unaltered Augsburg Confession and Luther's Catechism were viewed as definitive expositions of Lutheran doctrine, and normative authority was ascribed to the Book of Concord. But one group of Ohio Lutherans took issue and in 1840 established the English Synod. They disagreed about the language for one thing since they saw many of their young people being spirited away by the revivals in the English-speaking churches. They also viewed meticulous adherence to the Augsburg Confession as a violation of the Lutheran principle of liberty of conscience and essentially ascribed to the Smucker position. This conflict in Ohio would spread through the church and dominate the theological dialogue for half a century.

The immediate consequence was, as I said earlier, the establishment of two institutions, only a day's journey apart—Capital University in 1850 and Wittenberg College in 1845. Both institutions included seminaries and for both the primary motivation was provision of an educated clergy representing their respective viewpoints. Wittenberg was designed and consciously influenced by the American model of the liberal arts college. This would be the first Lutheran institution in North America to be so shaped, while Capital would follow the model of the preparatory school and seminary and their aspirations pointed toward the German university model.

Meanwhile, in Pennsylvania there were theological stirrings as well which led rather directly to the formation of new educational institutions. By the 1850s Benjamin Kurtz felt that Gettysburg Seminary had become too formal and confessionally bound. He and Samuel Smucker argued for a revision of the Augsburg Confession. Except for three small synods in Ohio, their proposals were roundly rejected by the General Synod.

Kurtz' antagonist, Frederick A. Muhlenberg, felt that Gettysburg was too Americanized and not confessional or German enough. Kurtz and his followers were to establish what came to be known as the Missionary Institute at Selinsgrove, Pennsylvania, an institution which would further their views and lead eventually to the establishment of Susquehanna University. Muhlenberg and his allies would establish a college named after its founder at Allentown, Pennsylvania. The primary goal of Muhlenberg College would be to assure a supply of well-educated pastors, to conserve the ethnic heritage of German settlers, to introduce students to the classical studies constituent of the liberal arts, and to advance the cause of confessional Lutheranism.

The next wave of Lutheran heritage institutions was to trace its theological origins to old world struggles rather than the American experience. For example, the Missouri Synod Concordia system had its origins in Saxony. There had been a revival of Lutheran confessionalism in Germany during the Reformation anniversaries which were celebrated between 1817 and 1830. In the 1840s many Germans fled Saxony because of religious oppression. One of them was Martin Stephan from Dresden. He was a strong advocate of confessionalism and pietism. He led a band of immigrants to Missouri, and one of the first things they did was to establish a school. It was really a grade school–high school combination, but its vision was the preparation of pastors and teachers for the church who would uphold confessionalism and the use of the German language and who would oppose rationalism and unionism. The synod itself would exercise direct ownership and control over what would become a system of schools, colleges, and seminaries. This system was the only one of its kind in American Lutheranism. It produced a well-educated and like-minded clergy and became an effective instrument in maintaining orthodoxy. Some idea of the significance of the system is indicated by 1984 statistics which indicate that there were 1,705 elementary schools, seventy high schools, thirteen colleges, and four seminaries enrolling 200,000 students, staffed by 10,000 teachers.

Another major influence in the second German immigration to America was Johann Conrad Wilhelm Loehe, whose missionary interest led him and his followers in Germany to make a substantial commitment to missionary and educational activity in the new land. And, after a falling out with the Missouri Synod over the doctrine of ministry, Loehe's followers established their own educational enterprise for the preparation of teachers and pastors first in Saginaw, Michigan, then in Dubuque, Iowa, and then "in the uttermost parts of the earth" as Wartburg College became the most peripatetic of all Lutheran colleges.

One of the most unique ventures in education occurred in 1852 with the establishment of Illinois State University. This was not the public institution which now exists, but a private one. And it was established with the cooperation of several Lutheran groups including Germans, Norwegians, and Swedes. Its goal was the preparation of pastors, but almost immediately after its formation concerns emerged about its orthodoxy. In 1860 Lars B. Esbjorn, one of the professors, pulled out and took the Swedes and Norwegians with him to establish what was to become Augustana College and Seminary. It would have two departments, preparatory and theological. Its opening enrollment consisted of ten Norwegians, ten Swedes, and one "American." But even that effort at Scandinavian cooperation was premature, and in 1864 the Norwegians determined that they wanted their own college and seminary with a narrow, more simplified course of study than the one offered at Augustana. That led to the establishment of Augsburg Seminary and Marshall Academy in Marshall, Wisconsin, in 1864.

Next we pick up the story of Luther College. As with the German immigrants, the Norwegians all did not see things alike. One group was somewhat anticlerical and strongly evangelical. They were called Haugeaners (named after the Norwegian reformer Hans Nilsen Hauge), and they would move their educational undertakings from Illinois State to Augustana Seminary, then to Marshalltown, and eventually to Red Wing and Minneapolis. The other principal group of Norwegian Lutherans was more liturgical, clerical, and confessional. They organized themselves into the Norwegain Synod in 1853 and established Luther College in 1861. They were strongly committed to academic and doctrinal integrity and had looked to the German-sponsored Concordia Seminary initially for their clergy until the Civil War came along—a story we will pick up later. But for now it is sufficient to note that Luther was the first of the Norwegian Lutheran colleges. It, like its German and Scandinavian predecessor institutions, was established for the purpose of providing and educating clergy representative of a particular theological perspective and/or style of ministry.

As the first of the Norwegian Lutheran institutions, Luther, like Gettysburg among the German heritage institutions, would provide leadership and faculty resources to a number of Norwegian heritage institutions that followed. For example, Luther contributed two presidents to St. Olaf as well as ten of its first fourteen faculty members. In addition, the founding presidents of both Concordia and Pacific Lutheran University were graduates of Luther College.

To pick up the thread of theological origins, we move next to St. Olaf College. Established in 1874, it was essentially a high school. What was unique is that it was co-educational from the beginning and its educational goal was to educate leaders for all of church and society, not just clergy. While some earlier colleges had made similar educational claims concerning their educational mission, St. Olaf succeeded in carrying out that mandate of its founders.

St. Olaf's college status and direction was to emerge from another theological battle, this one over predestination. (The followers of C. F. W. Walther of Concordia Seminary believed that the individual believer was predestined *into* faith, solely on the basis of God's grace and merit and the merit of Christ. Opponents said no, predestination takes place *in view of* individual faith which has been foreseen by God.) This conflict led to all sorts of realignments among Norwegian Lutherans and the establishment of the anti-Missouri Brotherhood, a group which asked St. Olaf to initiate a college program in 1886 and made use of the college's classrooms for its own seminary operation. So, again, theological battles explain in a significant way the early life of St. Olaf College.

The role of theological presuppositions in the establishment of colleges and seminaries is illustrated in Danish heritage institutions as well. Bishop Nicolai Grundtvig and his followers in Denmark did battle with the rationalists and encouraged the ministry of the laity. Grundtvig emphasized living faith and the positive potential of life, and he encouraged both cultural and spiritual awakening. On the other hand, Vilhelm Beck was the leader of a pietistic, Inner Mission movement that stressed the subjective elements of Christianity including conversion and sanctification. He and his followers took a narrower view of culture and a more pessimistic view of the world and nature. These contrasting views were transmitted to the new land and led to conflicts which would result in the establishment of separate Danish synods. The Inner Mission people established Dana College and Seminary in 1884, and the Grundtvigians established

Grand View College and Seminary in 1896. These seminaries persisted until the middle of the century with Trinity Seminary merging with Wartburg Seminary in 1956.

While there are additional proofs which could be brought forward, those cited are sufficient to indicate the very substantial role of theological intention and conflict in the establishment of Lutheran colleges in each of the ethnic families. Indeed, in most cases colleges were the handmaidens of, and coupled with, seminaries. In most cases the principal purpose for their establishment was provision of a clergy who would effectively carry forward a certain point of view.

But theological conflicts and intentions do not tell the whole story of the origins of Lutheran higher education. Social and political factors played a significant role in a number of cases. In the case of most institutions, the preservation of ethnic values and traditions was a major role in their establishment. Indeed, the reasons Illinois State University and the early Augustana effort failed included their inability to adequately respond to ethnic particularities. But other social and political factors were also at work in the establishment of colleges and universities. For example, Wittenberg University was established by Germans who were concerned that their young people were being proselytized by the English-speaking, revivalist groups. And so, in part, Wittenberg's commitment to both an American model of education and instruction in English was a response to the culture in which it found itself.

Not everyone responded to that American experience in the same way. The ministerium of Pennsylvania was concerned that the cultural influences of the New World were weakening the faith and life of their people, and so they established a seminary in Philadelphia and a college in Allentown which would preserve the use of the German language and, in that way among others, resist the secularizing influences of that day. The creation of Capital University reflected some of the same insecurity about cultural influences in the New World.

But the Luther story I hinted at earlier is perhaps the most interesting illustration of the role of social and political factors in the creation of a college. I noted earlier that by the mid-nineteenth century, the Norwegians had broken up into synods over disagreements—principally about matters of polity. The Norwegian

Synod was formed, and it established an alliance with Concordia Seminary of the Lutheran Church–Missouri Synod for the preparation of its pastors. Lauraitz Larsen occupied the Norwegian professorship at Concordia beginning in 1859. But some Norwegian farm boys from Wisconsin came home reporting that their seminary professors were sympathetic to slavery, and Norwegian Synod lay people asked Professor Larsen for an explanation. He hesitated, but then prepared an article in which he substantially endorsed the southern argument from Scripture, that slavery itself is not a sin. His argument was not persuasive. At a convention nine days later the synod met and determined that it should open its own school. Then the clergy argued that the synod should continue its affiliation with Concordia until enough money had been collected to fund a new school. But the lay people would have none of it. The clergy tried to push through a resolution on "what the Scriptures teach regarding slavery" and were surprised again by a heavily negative vote from the lay delegates. So Luther College was established as a direct consequence of the social conscience of the laity over the issue of slavery.

Another less glamorous example of the role of social factors is the Augsburg–St. Olaf imbroglio. This did not have anything to do with the creation of either college, but it had a great deal to do with their histories. In 1890 several Norwegian groups aligned together because they held common positions in the predestination conflict. They formed the United Norwegian Lutheran Church and determined that St. Olaf would be their college and Augsburg would be their seminary. The leaders of Augsburg at that time were Georg Sverdrup and Sven Oftedal, men who led Augsburg College and Seminary for forty years. Sverdrup had his own ideas about college education and did not think that St. Olaf measured up. Besides, he and Oftedal smelled a conspiracy and so they fought the deal tooth and nail and eventually resigned from this new church. Years of litigation ensued and a "Friends of Augsburg" group was formed to support the institution. Those friends eventually organized the Lutheran Free Church, the first example of a college serving as a progenitor of a church.

The stubbornness and, in retrospect, lack of foresight on the part of Sverdrup and Oftedal were costly for St. Olaf in the short term and for Augsburg in the long term. As a consequence, Augsburg suffered from too small a constituency and too few students through most of its early history. Indeed, it would not be until the middle of the twentieth century that it would receive full accreditation—all of which proves the axiom that family fights are difficult, but church fights are worse.

A third factor in the shaping of Lutheran higher education was educational vision. The early German colleges and seminaries, with the exception of Wittenberg, were organized around the German model with the combination of high school/college/seminary preparatory program with heavy doses of language, history, and theology. The Missouri vision was perhaps most unique because it was modeled very much on the German gymnasium and it involved a vertically integrated system beginning with parochial grade and high schools followed by junior colleges, senior colleges, and seminaries.

Another unique educational vision was that of Augsburg College. Oftedal and Sverdrup had strong opinions about how education should be organized. They established a nine-year classical program with three levels: the first was preparatory, the second was in Greek, and the third level was seminary education. It was really the only one of its kind among the Midwestern Lutheran colleges and, while it had been their intention to include programs for the laity, that aspect never caught on. So what may have been a first-rate program for the preparation of pastors did not respond to the educational needs of lay people in a growing and bustling city and hence the influence of the Augsburg program was quite restricted.

The American liberal arts model, of which Wittenberg was the first Lutheran example, provided the initial pattern for most of the late nineteenth and early twentieth century institutions, and the eventual pattern for all of the colleges including, more recently, the Missouri system.

Another distinguishing expression of the Lutheran educational vision was the academy movement. The Norwegians, Swedes, and Danes found that secondary education was a weak link on the frontier and beginning in the 1870s a total of seventy-five academies were established across the Midwest, Pacific Northwest, and Canada. As public secondary education became accessible, most of these institutions disappeared but the heartiest, or most strategically placed, among them were transformed into colleges. Gustavus Adolphus, St. Olaf,

Bethany, Concordia, Pacific Lutheran, and Upsala all originated as academies or normal schools. In sum, there were people with special visions about education who managed to rally enough people around them to launch their dreams. Each vision was unique, and the fact that one mode merged as dominant makes the alternate visions no less important in telling the story.

A final factor which played a major role in the establishment of Lutheran colleges was simply the migration of Lutherans across the continent. The German heritage colleges in the South and the Norwegian and Danish heritage colleges in the Midwest and Northwest all reflected the movement of Lutherans. Their itch for education led them to establish colleges along the way and only occasionally with help from their parent synod—as in the case of Midland Lutheran College. The college planting story of the immigrants is one of faith active in sacrifice. One story might illustrate—the early story of Pacific Lutheran and its founder, Bjug Harstad. Harstad had started three academies in North Dakota in the 70s and 80s. He decided to do the same thing in the Pacific Northwest in the 90s. He met a real estate promoter who said, "Have I got a deal for you!" His deal was a land development near Tacoma. He would make one hundred acres of that development available to the college, and the college would receive a ten percent commission on all lots sold plus a $10,000 bonus if all the lots were sold. What a deal! The sale of lots was brisk at the outset and so ground was broken for a five-story building capable of accommodating 248 students. Then the economy turned sour, and the sale of lots bogged down and eventually collapsed. Three years into the building project, funds ran out. The Norwegian Synod was asked to take over the school but, after looking at the books, would have none of it. Harstad was disconsolate that the land scheme had cost many of his good friends money and so, in a last-gasp, bizarre event, he spent eighteen months tramping the gold fields of Alaska in search of a great bonanza. Harstad's successors would eventually persevere and so a long story turned out to be a good story, but it should be noted that there were probably more failures than successes in the story of Lutheran higher education.

Those are some of the highlights of the story—where the colleges came from and why. And that leads us to ask, "What shall we make of it? How shall we assess the role and influence of these colleges?" First of all, we can say that the colleges have kept faith with the Lutheran tradition of taking education seriously, initially for pastors and then for laity as well. Indeed, I would submit that the colleges have been one of the major expressions of the American commitment to the Lutheran idea of vocation. As noted previously, these colleges have been bastions for liberal arts education and that too is a reflection of Reformation heritage with appropriate adaptations to the American scene. That does not mean that all of the colleges are alike in program scope or content, only that in every case the liberal arts are both the educational core and the philosophical framework for the educational program.

The colleges have provided clergy for the church. Initially it was almost their exclusive function, and through most of our history they provided nearly all of the students at our seminaries. And while that situation has changed in recent decades, the colleges continue to be a major source of candidates for ministry.

The colleges have also been conservators of culture. In particular, the Lutheran commitment to art, drama, and music reflects and perpetuates a rich heritage. Many of these colleges have gained national and, in some cases, international reputations for the quality of their cultural programs. The colleges have also been conservators of ethnicity. At the outset, it was a matter of self-preservation and security and at midstream in our histories it may have been a sign of parochialism. But in the current milieu, it is most often a matter of serious academic reflection and assists both the constituencies and students of these colleges in taking their own history seriously within the framework of a multicultural, multihued world.

The colleges have also provided a special model of Christian community, a community that includes elements of worship, social interchange, and mutual support. There is an almost mysterious bonding that takes place among our faculty and students—call it "the work of the Spirit" if you will. It is a bonding which we believe our students replicate in the communities to which they move in their sojourns. And such "habits of the heart" as these are not to be taken lightly in these last years of this century.

Finally, the colleges have provided the church with a special laboratory for discipleship. Whether it was the slavery issue in the 1860s, the League of Nations debate in the 1920s, the civil rights issues of the 60s, the Vietnam crisis of the 70s, or the rural and Third World challenges of the 80s, the church colleges have been front line places for dialogue and action. Colleges are criticized for knowing more about thought than action, but that has not inhibited them from either. In a significant way society and the church expect our campuses to be places of thought and action where new ideas emerge and are tested, where students bump up against the tensions between faith and action and the attendant anxieties. While our campuses are not as some call it "the real world," they serve the church by being a laboratory of that world, a place for the preparation of disciples.

Finally, I note that whereas colleges were once lively places and expressions of theological conflict in the church, that is no longer true in the same way. Why is that so? Many reasons I suppose—because colleges and seminaries are separate from one another, because theological disputes are more civil, and perhaps because Lutherans have become more homogenized in a theological sense. That is not to say that theological issues are not part of the agenda that gives liveliness and, in some cases, particularity to our places. The debates about the scope of salvation, sacramentalism, and specific genres of theology—those debates are part of the flow of our academic and religious life. And what is true of colleges is likewise true, I suspect, of theological seminaries of the church.

One consequence of the separation of seminary and collegiate education is the decline of dialogue between colleges and seminaries. I assess that as a loss. I do not mean that there is no dialogue—your professors spend some time professing on our campuses—but there is, unfortunately, less flow in the other direction. Likewise, our presidents, deans, and board members have scarcely any dialogue or common agenda, and that, I submit, is a loss to colleges, seminaries, and the church.

This nearly completes my visit to the heritage of the colleges, but I will borrow a few more minutes of your time to explore the future of Lutheran colleges and, more particularly, the colleges of the soon-to-be-incorporated Evangelical Lutheran Church in America (ELCA).

Richard Solberg says that colleges have been the most influential educational vehicle of the Lutheran tradition in North America. If that was true in the past, what about the future? The answer, I believe, turns on at least five factors. The first will be how this new church understands its mission. The constitution of the ELCA sets out mission in these words:

> The Division of Education, in response to the church's commitment to be in mission in higher education, shall encourage, assist, and sustain the colleges and universities of this church, both individually and as a community of institutions.

Those are encouraging words for colleges of this new church. They identify college education as integral to the mission of the church just as surely as foreign missions, evangelism, social ministry, and theological education. So, at its birthing, this new church does not see education as a satellite operation but as an essential dimension of what this church is. The proposed constitution details a number of ways in which the ELCA intends to take seriously that commitment. The living out of this commitment will be a major factor in determining the future influence of Lutheran colleges.

A second key factor determining the course of colleges in the life of the ELCA will be our vision of education. Again, I read from the proposed constitution regarding the Division of Education:

> This division shall recommend policies for this church's relationship to colleges and universities. These policies shall be faithful to the Lutheran tradition that its colleges are an essential expression of God's mission in the world; faithful to the will of God as institutions providing quality instruction in religion and the lively ministry of worship, outreach and service; faithful to the world by preparing leaders committed to truth, excellence and ethical values; and faithful to students in their dedication to the development of mind, body and spirit.

This is a remarkable vision. I note especially that it reflects the confessions of the church in its commitment to the creative order, to reconciliation and community. And this vision also reflects a holistic concept of life in its commitment to the development of mind, body, and spirit. This vision is a challenge to the colleges, and our future will depend in large measure upon our ability to claim and exemplify this lively and faithful goal.

A third factor determining our future as ELCA colleges will be the relationship between our institutions and the church. We colleges of the American Lutheran Church have not seen ourselves as church-related colleges but as colleges of the church. That difference is not merely semantic; it is, I submit, theological. We have seen ourselves as part of the body of Christ, the church, and not appendages to it. Our rhetoric has never been "us and them" but rather "we and ours." Follow our language in these coming years to see which conception comes to characterize the relationship, for it will be a strategic sign.

A related question is how we embody the relationship of church and college. In recent decades we have noted the decline in the number of Lutherans served by our colleges—now less than fifty percent of the aggregate enrollments of the colleges of the ELCA. There have also been changes in governance that have not necessarily strengthened church connections to colleges. And in the new church, regions will assume a new role in brokering the formal aspects of the relationship between individual colleges and the church. All of which says to me that individual colleges will have more responsibility for the relationship between college and church than they have had in the past. That will be a challenge, a challenge which many of us believe we are in a splendid position to accept, given the tradition of strong relationship.

The fourth key factor in describing the future will be the coherence of our college communities. We are more diverse and inclusive than we have ever been. Indeed, some are more diverse from a religious point of view than they care to be. In other cases, institutions like my own are less inclusive from an ethnic point of view than we would like to be. That diversity represents, I suspect, both the breadth of our mission and the flow of our opportunities as institutions. In the midst of such opportunities we want to conserve the educational vision of our colleges, and that will require coherence in the community—coherence among curriculum goals, community values, and religious commitment and practice. It is a challenge not to be taken for granted. Robert Bellah has written about the special opportunity for church and college communities to model a coherence of caring values and deeds. Not surprisingly, coherence is a lively topic of discussion on the campuses of church colleges these days. We wonder what it ought to mean and how its benefits are to be secured in this pluralistic time. I submit that an axiom found in the history of Norwegian Lutherans might serve us well as we ponder this question. That axiom is "firmness at the center and flexibility at the periphery." It is a way of saying that we must pursue the search for coherence with both faithfulness and grace.

A final factor in my assessment of the future of colleges in the ELCA is the faculty and staff. They are the most important factor of all, for they are the ones who embody the mission, who bring the vision to life, and who express coherence in our communities. In a convocation address on our campus last fall, Russell Edgerton, the president of the American Association of Higher Education, told a story about a man who came upon two medieval stonecutters and asked, "What are you doing?" The first replied, "I am squaring a bloody stone." The second looked up and said, "I am building a cathedral." They were doing the same task, but the second stonecutter saw his work in terms of the larger whole. If we are to keep faith with the heritage we have revisited, we will require cathedral builders—people who look after the education of body, mind, and spirit; men and women who seek coherence in the lively dialogue between faith and learning, religion and life; stewards who know the redemptive experience of membership in the body of Christ—for that is what building cathedrals is all about.

CHAPTER SIX

Through a Glass Darkly:
Mission in the Twenty-First Century

1991 Lutheran Educational Conference of North America

In the late 1980s the academy began an engaging discussion about the strengths and weaknesses of the rationalistic/scientific method that was then the icon of the academy. While music, literature, philosophy, religion, spirituality, and the arts offered alternative ways of knowing and understanding truth, they had been eclipsed by the hegemony of the scientific method. A critique of this method was perhaps overdue. My own reading at the time convinced me that Lutheran liberal arts colleges needed to mine their tradition and be a part of this conversation. So when I was invited by the Lutheran Educational Conference of North America to address their annual meeting, I agreed to do so. This address was not so much a critique of the scientific method as it was a call to address some matters for which that method lacked tools—thus the consideration devoted to values, religious life, intellectual paradigms, and mission.

Let me begin by limiting the subject of these reflections: First, they are addressed to the mission of Lutheran colleges and universities, and this essay will focus on educational issues that are intrinsic to colleges of this general character. Such issues as assessment, college finance, diversity, financial aid, and global studies, while worthy in their own right, are addressed competently in a variety of educational forums and will not be included in these reflections. Second, I acknowledge the diversity represented in the Lutheran family of colleges and universities—diversity in self-understanding, in church relationship, and in conception of mission. Accordingly, it is expected that readers will interpret and evaluate these reflections through a variety of lenses.

I believe that the mission of Lutheran colleges and universities in the next century will be shaped in response to five key changes: the changing place of values in our society, the changing intellectual paradigm, the changing patterns of religious life, the changing sense of mission within our institutions, and the changing relationships between college and church. I believe we are experiencing, and will continue throughout the 1990s to experience, a "sea change" in Lutheran higher education. Some elements of that sea change are discernible and others are not, for which reason we can only expect to envision the future "through a glass darkly."

The values change in our society is well chronicled. The national culture of media, commerce, politics, and education sets the agenda. What Michael Novak described as the "local culture" of religious, ethnic, family, and neighborhood experiences and values has been in decline for some time. Robert Bellah and others have described the resulting ascendancy of individualism and materialism. The church, especially the main line churches, and our colleges have all been affected. The academy in which most of our faculty was prepared experienced the ascendancy of the enlightenment and scientism which, in turn, cast doubt about the efficacy of values as an appropriate intellectual category. So, reflecting the inclination of the prevailing culture and its intellectual style, values categories and related expectations were jettisoned in institutions all across the land. Some of that activity was past due, and some of it was an over reaction. The impact of those changes on the academy has been analyzed by everyone from the controversial Allan Bloom to the Carnegie study on campus climate.

But places with traditions, constituencies, and missions like ours could never quite abandon a concern for values. That emphasis runs too deep. It is embodied in our faculties, our parents, our students, our church, and our constituencies. So in respect to keeping our long-held values, we fought a rear-guard action in the academy and in the culture.

Now, things have begun to change. The Carnegie Commission, among other sources in the culture, is urging the rehabilitation of community as a value. The call for civic responsibility comes from all corners of the land. When civil libertarian Norman Lear becomes an advocate of values education in the schools and deals with value issues on primetime television, then you know that some corner has been turned. Similarly, the data from the annual freshman survey of the Higher Education and Research Institute, as well as our own campus experiences, point to encouraging signs among our students.

The response of the academy to all of this is a little hard to sort out. There are national conferences on values, foundation grants, pilot projects, and across the curriculum programs, but it is perhaps too early to separate form from substance, trend from permanence. What I believe is pivotal in the mission of our colleges in the next decades is that we continue to bring our unique tradition to bear in these matters. In 1989 William M. Sullivan, a member of the team that produced *Habits of the Heart,* offered the opinion that values in our society are driven by management, feeling, and style rather than any fundamental commitments. The result is a disordered value system.

It seems to me helpful to acknowledge those characteristics that distinguish colleges like ours in approaching value issues. I believe we have the capacity to make a unique contribution to this matter. First of all, in dealing with such issues, we begin with conviction while much of society tends to be preoccupied with technique. I have been impressed by Parker Palmer's view that knowing begins with love. Love is what binds up the world and directs behavior. That is where we begin as Christians, with God's love toward us, to which we respond with love for God, love for one another, and love for the world. Palmer says we often begin with the facts of human life and behavior, and surround them with ethics and mandates to shape the behavior of, say, engineers, industrialists, politicians, educators, and students. The emphasis is on technique. There is a lot of that going on today in the development of courses, programs, and workshops to address specific ethical behaviors. But where it must begin and where, it seems to me, we begin distinctly, is with conviction. One of those convictions is, as I say, the conviction of love. Another unique Lutheran conviction has to do with our understanding of human nature and the Gospel. The reality of original sin keeps us diligent, the news of the Gospel keeps us hopeful, and grace enables us to navigate the dialectic between the two. Yet another unique conviction for Lutherans is grounded in our concept of vocation which puts value behavior in an appropriate religious category.

Another distinction in our approach to value issues is that it is communal rather than individual. Society, left at sea because it lacks common anchorage or conviction increasingly is made up of individuals making choices determined by some private, internal reading of right and wrong, good and bad. We hear that from those who speak the loudest on both sides of the abortion debate, and we hear it from our own students in their reflection on critical issues. It is not that they (or we) are not "good" people; it is that they (and we) are creatures of an age in which we lack moorings and so we look for them on the inside. What characterizes our tradition as church and college is that we look to the community—the community of faith, the community of learners and believers. With love for God and each other as our conviction, we look to each other in making ethical decisions and to our common value heritage in the experience of Israel, the teachings of Jesus, and the traditions of the church. Arvid Sponberg of the Valparaiso faculty, writing in the February 1989 *Cresset*, emphasized the importance of community in transmitting values. He referred to a conclusion of William Perry's research that for college students who choose to invest their lives through commitments choose the most important source of support—their family.

Another way of describing a Lutheran approach to values is to distinguish between reflection and engagement. I am not, of course, talking about mutually exclusive activities. We simply must avoid the typical "two kingdoms" mistake. But I note that a good deal of what occurs in society and much of higher education leaves off at reflection. We have a tendency to analyze and categorize, and we do it well. But we often assume that our work is done at that point. What is distinctive about the Lutheran habit is engagement. In a thoughtful piece on vocation in the December 1988 *Cresset*, Dr. Ernest Simmons pointed out that the Lutheran tradition is not dualistic but dialectic. We cannot leave ethics in a box. We want to understand in terms of the way ethics engages flesh and blood, real-life issues. On our campuses we spend time on that in faculty seminars; in conferences on faith and learning; in innovative learning and service programs; and in working out our common life in residence halls, governance, and co-curricular life. Engagement is distinctive in our approach to values issues.

Finally, we can distinguish the approach of our tradition by contrasting specialized and holistic methodologies. Again, it is the temptation of society, and Lutherans too, to assign values to a court, a prosecutor, or a special commission, and feel that somehow the job will be done. The academy often takes a similar approach by establishing codes, appointing committees, establishing curricula, and, again, assigning responsibility to given departments and professors. In our best moments we recognize that value behavior is the business of the whole. We may have specialized courses here and there, owing to the existence of specialized bodies of knowledge and methodologies in disciplines like philosophy, religion, and business. But that is not, for us, even the beginning of the beginning, for virtually every discipline and area of campus life is a place of value behavior and value generation. Every professor and staff member works on value issues in her or his professional life, and we all bring that experience to the community.

In the decade ahead, a time of value confusion and questing, there will be considerable babble about values education, but there will also be fresh opportunities for institutions from our tradition. Many of our institutions are on the cutting edge in modeling values education. Given that tradition, we may become "little platoons" serving as leaven in the larger society.

A second change that we will deal with in this decade is the emerging intellectual paradigm. These observations are shaped by writings on the subject by Parker Palmer and Arthur DeJong. Most of our faculty members were nurtured by an intellectual paradigm sometimes described as Cartesian–Newtonian. It sees the world as a closed structure, rules out the transcendent, and tends to separate fields of knowledge from one another. Objectivism is its reigning epistemology. In Palmer's view, this paradigm has tended to be anti-communal in that it destroys the capacity for relationship and for community.

A newly emerging intellectual paradigm draws on the work of feminists, the new sciences, and ethnic scholars. It does not ignore the objective, analytic, and experimental methodologies of the reigning paradigm, but it places them in a new context, to use Palmer's words, "a context of affirming the communal nature of reality itself."

The impulses for the new paradigm are both positive and negative. For example, the now well-documented world ecological crisis has illustrated the interdependence of scientific, economic, and political analyses in addressing the matter. (In a 1989 ELCA conference on the mission of the church, "The Year 2000 and Beyond," scholars from the sciences underscored the current predicament. Fausto Massimini, a cross-cultural psychologist from the University of Milan, spoke of the collapse of both Marxism and capitalism and the need to renew the emphasis on the spiritual. Gerald O. Barney, a physicist and director of the Institute for Twentieth Century Studies, spoke about threats to the environment and the need to engage the whole culture, including religion, if we are to survive the crisis. Solomon Katz, University of Pennsylvania anthropologist, said science and technology cannot do the job alone; human values and spirituality are indispensable.) The positive evidence of a new paradigm emerges from several quarters as well. Molecular biologists discovered that environments beyond the cell must be understood before the cell itself may be understood. The pioneering work of geneticist Barbara McClintock, more precisely her theory of transposition, pointed the way to this new revolution in biology.

Palmer describes the new paradigm as transcendent, holistic, and communal. It is transcendent in both practical and symbolic ways. Practically, the new paradigm speaks to the divisions we have developed among disciplines on our campuses—most especially the way we have tended to isolate and segregate value and religious questions, and also the way we have permitted the compartmentalization of campus life into academic, social, and religious categories with insufficient serious, substantive dialogue. While our catalogs have spoken of integration, we have often assumed that the agents of that integration will be the students themselves. Indeed, the reigning epistemology of separation has played right into the hands of the worst tendencies of Luther's Two Kingdom's paradigm and the inclination to separate rather than unite.

The new paradigm is also transcendent in a symbolic sense, and in this way the emergence of the new paradigm discussion seems almost providential to colleges like ours. For us the discussion of paradigm is not just a matter of epistemology but of mission. Joseph Sitler was one of the great apologists for the intellectual task of the church. He was always probing at the edge of knowledge in search of a new integration in service of the transcendent. As one of his interpreters put it: "Wholemindedness is a religious duty, because to come to God's world with anything less than an openness, curiosity, and thoroughness appropriate to the fabulously rich world of which we are a part, reduces our ability to see and serve the Creator." So the Gospel gives the academic enterprise its transcendent motive, and reconciliation provides a transcendent model for knowing. All of this does not limit the academy to religious or theological matters; rather, it compels us to test knowledge wherever it may be found.

A second characteristic of the new paradigm is that it is holistic. Palmer speaks of this as the concept of "whole sight," a vision of the world that unites the eye of the heart and the eye of the mind, the affective and the cognitive, the spiritual and the material. The ascendance of the Cartesian-Newtonian paradigm led us to separate knowledge from its roots and its relatives, and then describe as "soft" those disciplines that could not operationalize, measure, or manipulate variables. Education began to retreat from encounter with personal development and repair to the safe harbor of what we called "intellectual development." As Ernest Boyer put it in his landmark study of undergraduate education in America, "The disciplines have fragmented themselves into smaller and smaller pieces, and undergraduates find it difficult to see patterns in their courses and to relate what they learn to life." But, as we know, the most serious issues that assail society and our own campuses do not bend to objectivist treatment, and so we find ourselves searching again for the connections and relationships, for the composition of the whole as well as the definition of its parts. One turns again to our religious heritage for models, to the Apostle Paul and his discussion of the many parts of the body, each important in itself but all interdependent and united in the same spirit.

Palmer sees community as the third characteristic of the new paradigm. He has discussed the contemporary problem of the estrangement between the knower and the known. He believes it is at the root of the collapse of community and accountability. Palmer proposes that community is both the means and ends of the new paradigm. As a means it involves collaboration among scholars and learners and an explicit effort to enter into the communities of those represented by "the facts" of history and science. And the desired end of learning motivated by love is community.

What Palmer and others argue for is not that we abandon the old paradigm, but that we place it in the context of the new. Then the objective will be seen in the context of the relational, analysis will be juxtaposed with synthesis, and experimentation will be seen in contrast to receiving and accepting reality as it is.

I believe that the most important consequence of the emergence of the new paradigm is to encourage us in our tradition. What is "new" about this new paradigm to Lutheran colleges is not its ideology of transcendence, for that has been articulated in the best of our tradition. The call for wholeness, for integration, and for community is, similarly, an echo of the Lutheran liberal arts tradition. Many of the pedagogical initiatives, while sometimes new to this era, are not unique. So what makes this paradigm new is not so much its content but its context, a context of social crisis, of intellectual malaise, and of new scholarly impulses. We are academies in a world newly aware of the limits of the reigning epistemology and in search of something better. We are academies in a world now more open to the transcendent, the spiritual, the human, and the communal. There is a growing awareness that, whatever we call it, the reigning paradigm is no longer adequate to the business of the world, the spirit of humans, and the call of the Creator. So it is context that occasions us to see some familiar method and content in a new way and to name it by a new name. Colleges like ours may be the most likely to apprehend and claim the "new paradigm," for our view of the world is transcendent and our call in the world is to love.

The third trend that I believe will influence our mission in the twenty-first century has to do with the changing patterns of religious life. In the research of Wade Clark Roof and others, we are informed that religious individualism is in the ascendancy in modern culture. In a Gallup poll, seventy-eight percent of the respondents believed that "one can be a 'good' Christian or Jew without going to church or synagogue." People are acting on that conviction, church affiliation and attendance are a problem, particularly in the mainline churches. Most of us can see its impact in our local congregations and the religious life on our campuses. This habit of community, so important to places like ours, is simply not what it once was. If it is hard to project much loyalty to the local congregation, think about the problems in maintaining loyalty to the more distant synod, college, and national church.

Another dimension of this individualism in church life is what Roof calls "the new voluntarism"—the tendency to seek out religious affiliation in terms of personal needs, not common needs or the mandates of the Great Commission. The thriving congregation, according to Lyle Schaller and our own experience, is the one that recognizes and responds to this consumer mentality. The church, or college, that fails to recognize this reality may expect to experience continuing shrinkage in membership and influence. We will need to be creative at this point to maintain the integrity of our tradition while responding to this reality of the age.

Still another dimension of individualism is subjective belief, the famous "Sheilahism" of Bellah fame: "You believe what you will, and I'll believe what I will, and everything is fine." This is a special challenge to churches and church-related institutions like ours, which emphasize the symbols of the faith, tradition, and continuity. Whether cause or consequence of subjectivism, another reality with which we must deal is the low level of religious literacy among our students. When it does not matter much what one believes in the culture, then confirmation and Bible study are perceived as being of marginal significance.

Both subjective belief and religious illiteracy underscore the importance of the content and form of religious worship, religious study, and community life at Lutheran colleges and universities. We can communicate to our students a religious tradition with mooring points beyond self. Holding up the symbols of our faith in worship is one of the most salutary things we can do, because we do so in the confidence that God promises to send his Spirit in, with, and through these instruments of grace. Our community traditions of care-giving are another means by which we pierce the walls of individualism and subjective belief in an existential way. We demonstrate that it is not normative for people in our places to suffer alone, to celebrate alone, to work alone, or to meet God alone. Education, worship, and community are strong resources in turning the tide for students who are products of an age of individualism.

Placed in juxtaposition to these trends is a new spirituality in our society and a new quest for community. This is the good news part of the story where our institutions are concerned. Wade Clark Roof tracks the disenchantment of the baby boomers with the organized church—two-thirds of them left. Many moved through lifestyle cycles and now seek spiritual meaning in their lives. Tired of materialism, science, and technology, they are now looking for religious reality in their lives. Perhaps this is what led Bill Moyers to predict that religion would be the story of the 1990s. To be sure, consistent with their devotion to individualism and the new voluntarism, people are looking for spiritual meaning consistent with their needs, and so, again, the mainline churches and institutions draw no "byes" in this game. But rather than becoming cynical, we should take heart in the fact that Lutheran colleges and universities have always legitimized and responded to those on a spiritual quest. Indeed, at our places we believe such a quest is the centering element in the whole process of education. That kind of holism is unique in our culture and a great resource to our students. It behooves us to cultivate this distinctive element of our credo and announce it for all to hear. For this, above all, makes our places unique in a culture increasingly starved for wholeness and spiritual meaning.

The fourth key issue shaping our colleges in the twenty-first century will be the sense of mission within our institutions. This analysis begins by reiterating the reality of the diversity among our institutions. While I shall comment in general terms, each college or university community will have to transcribe and test these views out of its own unique vision. In his *Sacred Canopy*, Peter Berger said that every institution has a "plausibility structure." That is, an institution stands for something and is plausible or viable to the degree that that "something" is kept alive in the hearts, minds, and lives of the members. The "something" we stand for is our mission, and we will remain viable to the extent that mission is claimed by us and we, in turn, are claimed by it. The "us" I have in mind is principally the leadership cadre of our places—trustees, faculty, and staff.

In an earlier era, and the date will vary depending upon institutional history, the mission of our colleges and universities was largely implicit. It was embodied in the faculty, most of whom had come out of the tradition or been fully grafted onto it. At many of our schools, mission was also implied and assumed by a fairly homogeneous church-related student body and constituency. The sense of identity with institutional mission was not, in most cases, either an intellectualized or self-conscious matter.

But now, in a world grown small, a society grown more fully secular, an academy shaped by scientism and disciplinary identities, in institutions that have grown more diverse, the sense of institutional loyalty and identity with mission is no longer implicit. The essays by James Burtchaell (*First Things*, April and May 1991) and George M. Marsden (*First Things*, January 1991) are sobering reminders of what has happened in many church-related institutions in America. Whether by design or cultural accident, we are more diverse and secular places. The core of our being as colleges of the church, these places where the quality of life and the intellectual quest are shaped by the Gospel, cannot be assumed.

I believe the key issue of mission for our church and our individual colleges is how well we will be able to articulate and transmit to our faculty and staff in an intellectually thoughtful way our distinctive ethos and logos. Several more specific challenges are implied. The research effort by Richard Solberg and Merton Strommen a decade ago gave us some indication about the kind of faculty who are most likely to support our mission. The most important of those indicators are declared religious commitment and participating membership in an organized congregation. For that reason and others, it seems to me that we will want to make the most of each others' graduates and the graduates of other church-affiliated institutions when seeking to restock our faculties during the high turnover days just ahead for most of us. The ELCA's Data Link is one model—no sure thing, but an important beginning. I believe our denominational divisions for education could provide a great and strategic service by reviving some of the effective strategies of the 1960s when we offered fellowships and personal encouragement to graduates with special promise as faculty and staff for our institutions. Several of our core faculty came to us as a result of such efforts.

I acknowledge that these efforts, important as they are, will not be sufficient. We will need to hire more people from diverse religious traditions, and for those who are strangers to our tradition we shall need to provide systematic orientation to our communities. There are some creative ways in which strangers to our tradition may become full members of the family. We all have seen that happen. There are some excellent models among us. I am simply arguing that the new circumstances will make such efforts even more important for all of us. College presidents and academic deans will need to provide leadership on our campuses both by communicating the tradition to the community and by finding creative ways to educate and integrate those who are strangers to it. Together, through such ventures as Data Link, regular symposiums, and the activities of LECNA and the ALCF, the church and its colleges can perpetuate the tradition and build that critical mass of "believers" so essential to our faithfulness as institutions.

The final issue shaping the mission of the Lutheran colleges in the twenty-first century will be the changing relationships between college and church. Our churches these days are preoccupied with matters related to self-preservation. Financially, the colleges are perceived as being self-reliant, successful, and less in need of the churches' attention than other matters and missions. While our church leaders, in their reflective moments, acknowledge the history of church-abandoned colleges, the church nonetheless continues to move in that direction. We can and do argue vigorously about the high stakes for the church in this trend, that it can ill afford life without its colleges, yet the movement continues. Consequently, I would argue that the future of the church–college relationship will have more to do with the leadership and actions of the colleges than of the churches.

I acknowledge that the colleges' strong place in the church is still evident in some isolated counter actions. For example, in a recent effort in the ELCA to restructure college activities into a less central place, the colleges discovered that they had more friends than they expected, given the flow of bad news that had preceded this matter. Leaders and friends of the colleges worked hard, and they took responsibility for their relationship. They succeeded because of what they did and, more important, because scores of bishops and church council members were predisposed toward their cause and hence willing to listen and respond. Therein is some specific clue about our future—that is, our need to be engaged with these friends throughout the governance structure of the church who are in position to encourage and sustain our mission. We will need to do this both systematically and continually.

Let me shift this analysis of the relationship a bit. Most of what I have said about the flow of church decisions applies to the national expression of the church. It is, to be sure, extremely important. But of growing importance are the role and actions of the regional churches—more specifically, the synods, the districts, and the local congregations. In days when nearly all clergy were graduates of our colleges and the ethos of the national church was decidedly college-oriented, we could simply assume sympathy and support throughout the church. That is less true today both because our graduates make up a smaller percentage of the clergy roster and, again, because there is increased competition for church dollars and church loyalty. And, at least in the ELCA, we appear to be much more of a synodically and locally focused church than we once were. Synods are the resource gathering points; individual congregations that feel lots of space between themselves and a national structure representing five million members feel "connected" to their synod. Some of us have come out of a national model of college relationships and so have difficulty adjusting to this new reality. Some built-in tendencies toward parochialism go along with regionalism, a provincialism to which several Lutheran institutions may attest in their histories. But this analysis of a trend toward regionalism leads me to suggest that our colleges will need to find ways to cultivate and extend those relationships. Whether it be recruiting students or financial support or providing service in partnership ventures, I believe the action and the opportunities will, increasingly, be more regional for most of us. Some in our number, particularly those institutions which "live" alone in their region, have that figured out already and will have to mentor the rest. Other colleges and universities, due to both historical tradition and geographical overlap in the constituencies served, will have a more difficult time with this new reality. But, again, every institution has friends in these regional entities and will need to find ways to bring them into informed networks of support and action.

Finally, let me reiterate my conviction that the future of the relationship between colleges and the church will depend more on the leadership of the colleges than the actions of the church. Our histories, and in most cases our governing documents, are explicit about our intention to be colleges, servants and/or members of this body, this church. In view of the present flow of church history, presidents, faculties, trustees, and students will need to be more self-conscious about these matters than in the past. It is simply a matter of integrity and faithfulness.

Our colleges surely will not look and behave in the twenty-first century as they have in the last quarter of the twentieth. In the Lutheran tradition of engagement, staying the same would be a sign of unfaithfulness. And just as it did for our predecessors on the eve of this century, our confidence about the new century rests in the validity of our mission and the miracle of God's continuing work among us.

Works Cited

Robert N. Bellah, etal., *Habits of the Heart* (Berkeley: University of California Press, 1985).

Peter Berger, *The Sacred Canopy: Elements of a Sociological Theory of Religion* (Garden City, New York: Doubleday, 1967).

Allan Bloom, *The Closing of the American Mind* (New York: Simon and Schuster, 1987).

Ernest L. Boyer, *College, The Undergraduate Experience in America* (New York: Harper and Row, 1987).

The Carnegie Foundation for the Advancement of Teaching, *Campus Life: In Search of Community.* (Lawrenceville, New Jersey: Princeton University Press, 1990).

Arthur J DeJong., *Reclaiming a Mission* (Grand Rapids, Michigan: Wm. B. Eerdmans Publishing Co., 1990).

Harold H. Ditmanson, "Introduction," *Faith, Learning and the Church College: Addresses by Joseph F. Sittler*, Connie Gegenback, ed. (Northfield: Saint Olaf College, 1989).

Evelyn Fox Keller, *A Feeling for the Organism* (San Francisco: W. H. Freeman, 1983).

Parker J. Palmer, "Community, Conflict and Ways of Knowing," *Change*, September–October, 1987.

Parker J. Palmer, *To Know As We Are Known* (San Francisco: Harper and Row, 1983).

Wade Clark Roof and William McKinney, *American Mainline Religion* (New Brunswick and London: Rutgers University Press, 1989).

Richard W. Solberg and Merton P. Strommen, *How Church-related are Church-related Colleges* (New York: Division for Mission in North America, Lutheran Church in America, 1980).

CHAPTER SEVEN

The Future of Lutheran Higher Education

Inaugural Symposium
Luther College, November 22, 1996

In 1996 I was invited to present one of two keynote addresses at the Luther College symposium on the occasion of the inauguration of President Jeff Baker. I addressed two issues that were then on center stage in the academy—community and knowledge—and another that was only beginning to emerge in religious colleges—the idea of calling or vocation. I sought to address each of these topics out of the resources of the Lutheran theological and academic traditions. This address reflects my own deepening study of the Lutheran tradition, study that was enriched by the work of a task force on faith and learning at Concordia College. I believe that the Lutheran tradition had particular relevance to issues in the mid-1990s, but, I would add, it is a tradition whose relevance transcends specific eras and issues.

I am honored to speak to you today about the future of the Lutheran liberal arts college, a subject about which I am optimistic. Why? In part because I believe the Lutheran tradition is so relevant to the current milieu of the liberal arts and the society; in part because of the enthusiasm I see in the generation of teacher–scholars now entering our colleges; and, in part, my enthusiasm is undoubtedly a reflection of my own education, informed by so many lively and competent colleagues from places like this campus and my own, people in institutions which affirm and confess the tradition of faith and learning that undergirds our common enterprise.

Let me make my case for the future of the Lutheran liberal arts college with reference to three transcending issues: community, knowledge, and calling. That these three categories bear more than a dim reflection to Aristotle's categories of proof—ethos, logos, and pathos—surely reflects the habits of one trained in classical rhetoric. In the course of these remarks I will discuss three characteristics that can shape the future of Lutheran liberal arts colleges: that we are grounded in faith, committed to the world, and engaged in dialogue.

I. Community.

The crisis of community in our nation is well documented. Whether one looks at the crisis of our cities, the brokenness of community, the shallowness of our public square, or the tremors in family life, there is sufficient data for the argument that we may be on our way to "hell in a hand basket." Daniel Yankelovich tells us that four out of five Americans believe morality is in a state of decline in our country. To judge by the vigorous sales of William Bennett's *Book of Virtues,* many are very serious about these matters. It is clear that the American way of life and the Christian way of life are no longer synonymous, if they ever were. In our "culture of disbelief," religion has been marginalized and the biblical voice is now muted.

The crisis of community is more than a failure in virtue, it is also a problem of diversity. *E pluribus unum* (out of many one) is a slogan used to rouse and rally the miracle that is America. We were taught to affirm and celebrate diversity as children of God and citizens of this melting pot, American experiment. But lately, there is more *pluribus* than *unum* as diversity becomes difference, difference becomes discrimination, discrimination becomes prejudice, and prejudice becomes painful. In Putnam's language we are, increasingly, "bowling alone." Clair Gaudiani, president of Connecticut College, put it this way, "America is molting. Our democracy's social contract used to fit but no longer does because we have stretched, and we have not grown a new one. We feel pain and vulnerability."

There is in the tradition of the Lutheran liberal arts college an unwillingness to accept such a status quo. It begins with the story we live by, and that is the biblical story. In that story Jesus told us to feed the flock, and he warned us that if we neglect the neighbor in need, we have neglected God. In that story Paul first tells us of our freedom, our salvation by grace through faith. And then he goes on to say, in effect, therefore, "Do not be conformed to this world but be transformed by the renewing of your mind, so that you may discern what is the will of God, what is good and acceptable and perfect" (Romans 12:2). There it is: a call to virtue and justice, to neighborliness and equity in the community. Paul makes it clear that it will not be easy and it surely will not save our souls, but it is the road we are called to walk in faithful gratitude.

What is particularly Lutheran in our understanding of this story is that we have a nuanced view of virtue and change for we are *simul justus et peccator*, we are both saint and sinner. We live with this tension in our nature, this bondage of our wills, all of which means that we are called to be moral without being moralistic. Our theology of the cross tells us that pain, suffering, ostracism, and death itself are the expected experience of people of the way and so triumphalism is not our style.

But in addition to our nuanced view of change and virtue, the Lutheran rendering of the story presents us with a paradigm of engagement. Christ prayed for unity and Paul gave us the wonderful figure of one body with many parts, each part indispensable to the whole. Our paradigm of engagement is a paradigm of connection, of reaching out for the other. In his formulation of the two kingdoms, Luther gave us fodder for endless disputation, but there are also points of genius in it helpful to our times and places, and especially to making connections in an increasingly diverse society. Luther argued that we are to be engaged in the life of the earthly kingdom, a kingdom of such natural orders as family, community, and nation. Such places are subject to what he called the political use of the law, one purpose of which is to promote order, justice, and equity in the human community. This use of the law provides a bridge between Christians and people of other faiths with whom we are to work cooperatively in order to find common ground and to claim values around which a human community can flourish. George W. Forell argues that this understanding provides Lutherans with a distinctive insight and capacity for providing leadership and service in an increasingly multicultural world. This view allows, indeed requires, that believers transcend religious and political differences for the sake of the common good.

There are some obvious implications here for the common life of a Lutheran liberal arts college. If these communities are to be shaped by the biblical story, then worship, word, and sacrament are essential forms of nourishment in these places. We will nurture a nuanced but disciplined confidence in change. We will take virtue seriously and place it in its proper venue. We will be committed to finding points of unity in our increasingly diverse campus communities. We will construct curricula and pedagogies that prepare students for community building beyond the campus. These are the essentials of community building on our campuses, and they become gifts to the world as they come alive in our graduates.

Consider the impact of our student volunteers in the communities that surround our campuses and beyond. Their influence extends well beyond their proportion of the population. Think of the strategic deployment of our graduates in international venues, in service agencies, in educational institutions at all levels, and in corporate and financial centers. Their leadership and influence are profound because their work is the miracle of the leaven.

Or think about the church. Taken together Lutheran colleges and universities constitute one percent of the institutions of higher education in the nation and educate, at the outside, only eleven percent of ELCA youth. But three-quarters of the bishops, half of our missionaries and national staff, and forty percent of those elected to national boards and committees are graduates of our colleges, and this is not even to mention the impact of our graduates at congregational and synodical levels. In short, the leadership impact of our graduates far exceeds the small proportion of our membership who attend our colleges.

II. Knowledge.

But what will be the measure of truth in the community of the Lutheran liberal arts college? Surely no issue has engaged and enlivened the academy in recent years more than this one. George Marsden's analysis traces the evolution of the objective–modernist hegemony. What our passion for the utilitarian and objective did not crowd out of the academy, the new American mythos did. The humanities and theology were among the major casualties. We tried to make every branch of knowledge conform to the cannons of science under the illusion that there was some value free and indisputable truth out there somewhere. The power of this paradigm was felt in many church-related colleges that, in quest of academic respectability, sold their souls.

Let's be fair, the fruits of scientific study fueled the American economy, extended life expectancy, increased food production, produced incredible weapons of defense and destruction, and brought us to the moon. But meanwhile the fruits of science progressed, families crumbled, virtue was compromised, economic disequilibrium persisted, communities were divided, and—guess what—we discovered we were not so happy after all. Then along came the new biologists who argued that such truth as they discover is always contextual. Parker Palmer argued that there is an inevitable connection between the knower and the known, and feminist scholars and literary critics argued that all knowledge is perspectival in character. There is no Archimedean point, no truth with a capital "T." This is the hallmark of postmodernism (and a troublesome beginning point as well).

Well, I hasten to tell you, Lutherans can agree with much of this. Luther said reason was a great gift and it reigns in the earthly kingdom. While it is essential and helpful in dealing with matters of faith, it is not definitive. When we attempt to rationalize divine revelation, said Luther, reason becomes "the devil's whore." If we are simultaneously saint and sinner—guess what—our rational quest is fallible as well. But perhaps more to the point, James W. Voelz argues, "postmodernism, for all its excesses, is not our enemy, but a sort of friend, a late twentieth-century discovery that in so many ways, the perspective of the early church was right: Only believers can truly interpret the sacred books of God."

Yes, truth is perspectival, all of which makes us skeptical in a healthy way but not cynical. In the Lutheran tradition, knowledge is perspectival and it is grounded in the incarnation, the God who became flesh, the Christ in whom all things hold together, the Spirit who hears our groanings and yearnings. We begin our quest for truth with a connection to the creating, redeeming, and sanctifying God. That is the solid rock, the transcending truth, on which we stand. In this postmodern era, as my colleague Concordia philosophy professor

Gregg Muilenburg has observed, "We are . . . *invited* to see faith and learning as much more closely related than any self-respecting scholar would have admitted during the foundationalist era when knowledge was thought to have an indubitable basis."

There are implications here for the curricula of our institutions. If we are to bring our perspective to bear on the ongoing intellectual conversation, we need to be well grounded in our tradition. On our campuses that means attention to the Bible, theology, philosophy, and history, and the tools of communication, analysis, and language pertaining thereto.

A second distinctive characteristic of the Lutheran tradition that bears on this issue of truth is our commitment to the world. Ours is a culture-affirming tradition. Luther viewed humanity as one of God's great gifts, a matter to be enjoyed. Indeed, the world is the place of God's redeeming action, a place in which we are called to service. That being the case, we are obliged to know this world, to explore it in all its manifestations, and to go global, multilingual, and multicultural. It means a commitment to the sciences and to the arts—both fine and applied. If, taken together with my previous comments on curricula, all of this sounds like liberal arts education then do not be surprised, for that is the way Luther envisioned education for service in the earthly kingdom and it is the way Lutherans have approached education since the sixteenth century.

Another of the implications of our commitment to the world is a commitment to the place of reason and free inquiry. Gregg Muilenburg has observed that, while perspective may be unassailable in the current paradigm of the academy, "knowledge, on the other hand, is . . . (falsifiable) and welcomes, even demands rational challenges." Luther believed that reason should rule in the earthly kingdom and ought to have a special place there. At one point Luther is reported to have said, "How dare you not know what can be known?" Under his and his friend Melanchthon's leadership, the university at Wittenberg was a well-known place of unfettered free inquiry. Why not seek the truth? The Lutheran project is, in effect, to seek the truth wherever it may be found. There is no fear in that, for in our grounded perspective what we will discover is something new about what God has done. So the Lutheran tradition has insisted on intellectual integrity and academic excellence consistently and enthusiastically. It is why so many Lutheran colleges and universities in this country enjoy the prominence they do today. We are committed to knowing and understanding the world, God's creation, and our arena of service.

A third distinctive characteristic of the colleges of our tradition is the commitment to dialogue between our grounded perspective and the world. Niebuhr provided a typology of faith engaging the world that has stood well the test of time. At one end of the continuum is the model of Christ against culture and at the other end, the Christ of culture where Christianity is indistinguishable from the spirit and reality of the times. In the middle stands the Lutheran tradition of Christ and culture in dialectic and, often, in creative tension. As my colleague K. Glen Johnson put it: "Lutherans are bears for punishment. If there is a place for tension they go for it. Their theology is always a theology of distinctions, and that implies tension; law–gospel, faith–works, saint–sinner, finite–infinite, election–predestination, reason–faith. Here a distinction, there a distinction, everywhere a distinction." That is where our two kingdoms, *simul justus et peccator*, incarnational theology brings us.

What are the implications of this commitment to dialogue? With respect to the faith, we are willing to risk our story with energy and excellence and without fear or intimidation. With respect to the academy, we are eager to test and extend our grounded perspective by engaging in conversation with other perspectives. This means, in part, that we will seek knowledge concerning the gifts and traditions of other tribes and tongues and faiths with whom we share this world.

The Lutheran commitment to the dialectic between faith and world has concrete implications for our scholarship and our pedagogy. The Lutheran scholar challenged by the intricate connectedness of mind and spirit, living and believing, will explore those inevitable and fruitful connections. Likewise, the teacher will be sensitive to the hidden assumptions of faith that underlie every quest for knowledge as well as the inevitable implications for life and learning that flow from them. In an excellent essay at the Sittler Symposium in 1989, Mary Hull Mohr of Luther College observed:

We do not deserve to be colleges of the church if we do not have models on our campuses of people in every discipline who are consciously searching to understand how both the tradition and a liberal free kind of stance toward education are informed by the Christian faith and whose faith has the capacity to grow through a deeper understanding of the liberal arts.

Finally, all of our learning and teaching will be nurtured by the special freedom of grace. Even though reason may fail us or we may fail it, we press on and boldly so because out of our grounded perspective we have the assurance that in the final analysis our merit, our salvation, will not depend upon the validity of our intellectual formulations.

III. Calling.

The third of the transcending issues that presents a special opportunity for Lutheran liberal arts colleges is the issue of calling. We live in an age of uncertainty, an age of seekers. Consider the public interest in angels. The sale of books and symbols is brisk. Look at the popularity of books and self-help approaches to spirituality, religious and otherwise. In no less authentic a publication than *USA Weekend*, Bill Moyers recently observed: "Something is happening in America that as a journalist I cannot ignore. Religion is breaking out everywhere. Millions of Americans have taken public their search for a clearer understanding of the core principles of belief and how they can be applied to the daily experience of life." All of which is to say that people are looking for meaning, for purpose, for a calling.

Lutheran liberal arts colleges bring a particularly strong tradition to this yearning, and that is our view of vocation. We believe that the finite creature is the bearer of infinite reconciliation. That is our calling, and it is an inclusive calling. That is, it applies to all the baptized, not just those who bear holy office or holy order. It applies to all careers that are laudable and constructive, including doctor and teacher, farmer and housekeeper, street sweeper and maker of beer barrels. It is inclusive of life in family, community, church, and career. And it encompasses culture, work, and play.

At the heart of the mission statements of our Lutheran institutions one often finds this call to serve God in the world. In that sense, as institutions we acknowledge our calling to prepare students for vocation in the world. Here is good news for searchers, for people on a quest for substance and coherence and direction in life and education. Here is something irrepressible in our history and essential to our future.

In recent years teacher–scholars from our colleges have been gathering for conversations around the issue of "the Vocation of a Lutheran College." The conversation is invigorating as our teacher–scholars mine the rich tradition that is ours. In an address to the most recent conference on this subject, my colleague Robert Vogel said: "If there are graduates who wander across the stage at commencement, take a diploma, and aimlessly head into their futures, even if they graduate with highest honors, they have not taken from us the best we have to give, which is helping them to discover and claim their callings."

In every era of the histories of colleges like ours there have been material exigencies that called into question our future viability. We should not expect the future to be much different, and we will need to be both diligent and resourceful with respect to these matters. But I close as I began. The future of the Lutheran liberal arts college will depend on how effectively we live out our calling as places grounded in faith, committed to the world, and engaged in dialogue. This is the task that challenged the founders of these colleges and that has served so well the church and the world. Now, in our turn at the helm, I believe the tide is running in our direction. By God's grace we will be found faithful. *Soli Deo Gloria.*

Works Cited

"Faith and Learning in the Concordia Community: A Report to the Faculty" (Moorhead, Minnesota: Concordia College, 1995).

George Forell, "What's at Stake? The Place of Theology in the ELCA," *Lutheran Forum*, February, 1991.

Claire L. Gaudiani, "The Molting Pot: The Liberal Arts and Civil Society." Annual Report, Connecticut College, 1994-95.

K. Glen Johnson, "The Lutheran University: Mission, Task and Focus," Proceedings, Lutheran Educational Conference of North America, 1994.

George Marsden, *The Soul of the American University* (New York: Oxford University Press, 1994).

Mary Hull Mohr, "The Mission of the ELCA Colleges and Universities: A Liberal Arts Perspective," Conference Papers, The Joseph A. Sittler Symposium, Evangelical Lutheran Church in America, 1990.

Bill Moyers, *USA Weekend.* October 11-13, 1996.

H. Richard Niebuhr, *Christ and Culture* (New York: Harper and Brothers, 1951).

James W. Voelz, *What Does This Mean: Principles of Biblical Interpretation in the Post-Modern World* (St. Louis: Concordia Publishing House, 1995).

Robert Vogel, "Coherence—And Now What?" Unpublished manuscript, 1996.

CHAPTER EIGHT

The Soul of a Lutheran College

The 2000 Luther College Planning Symposium

In 2000, I returned to Luther College to participate in this important symposium. The audience of 150 included faculty, regents, alumni, students, and staff. I had multiple objectives in this address: First, through a fable I wished to convince those present that the future of the college should not be taken for granted. Second, I wanted to highlight some of the issues that would challenge the college. Third, I wanted to suggest ways in which the Lutheran tradition might be embodied in addressing various planning issues.

Let me begin with the fable of Christmas College. Christmas College was established by Swiss immigrants who were of the Zwinglian persuasion. They settled in central Iowa and established their college in 1895. The mission of the college, the first matter settled on by the founders, was to educate people who would lead lives of service dedicated to the glory of God. The college's motto was "*Soli Deo Gloria.*" The college was owned by the Zwinglian conference of central Iowa, established to serve the daughters and sons of the Zwinglian immigrants who wished to maintain their faith tradition. All the trustees were members of the Zwinglian family, as were all the faculty and every student. It was a liberal arts college located in a rural setting. In the early years it was slow going. Many colleges like Christmas College failed, but there were plenty of Swiss Zwinglian students and teachers to go around. It was a closely-knit community, and religious life was central to the place. There was not much talk about religious identity because it was simply taken for granted. A chapel was built on the campus before a library. Chapel attendance was, of course, required, and there were four courses in religion, one each year, that were central to the curriculum.

By the 1920s Christmas College was serving a new generation of students. World War I was over, and the great American melting pot was cooking away. It was then that Christmas College admitted its first non-Zwinglian students and hired a non-Zwinglian as a faculty member (although he was married to one). Most members of the faculty were graduates of Christmas College or one of its sister colleges, Easter College or Pentecost College. During the 1920s the faculty took some modest steps to diversify the curriculum when professional programs were added in accounting and education. Into the 1930s there was an emphasis on the professional preparation of faculty for, up until that time, there were few Ph.D.s who were essential for accreditation and institutional self-respect. Christmas College was caught up in the "Americanizing" of higher education that was occurring at that time all across the United States.

Fast forward to post-World War II. The good news is that Christmas College survived the Depression. That was only possible because of the loyalty of the members of the Zwinglian conference of central Iowa and the fact that the Zwinglians of that area prospered and multiplied. With the end of World War II there was a sudden growth in enrollment because of the returning veterans as well as others who were looking for a good education and better economic opportunities. Christmas College was, by slight degrees, becoming evermore Americanized, which some said was a good thing while others were not so sure. Dancing came to the campus in the 1950s, and the dress code grew more relaxed. Chapel was still required, and the campus remained a very intimate community.

In the 1960s Christmas College needed to expand its faculty when enrollment increased from five hundred students in 1946 to two thousand by 1970. By now the Zwinglians had become thoroughly Americanized, and many felt liberated. Many had moved away from central Iowa. Others had married non-Zwinglians and, not surprisingly, there were now more non-Zwinglian students, fewer Zwinglians, and many fewer graduates of Christmas, Easter, and Pentecost Colleges on the faculty. But it was still the case that every member of the faculty was affiliated with some Christian denomination. The curriculum was substantially expanded and improved, the languages and sciences prospered, and the humanities held their own. The faculty was much better credentialed, and there were many changes in campus life: Required chapel was dropped in the 1960s, and the number of services was reduced to three a week. The required courses in religion dropped from four to two over the decades.

In the early 1970s Christmas College faced a crisis. Enrollment had declined, public institutions were prospering and multiplying in central Iowa. The economy was harsh, and Christmas College was scrambling for students, faculty, and money. The Zwinglian conference of central Iowa, which had always provided Christmas College with substantial annual grants, reduced its financial support dramatically. In the 1970s Christmas College hired its first non-Zwinglian as dean, and the major emphasis in faculty hiring shifted from mission fit to professional credentials. The board of regents of Christmas College was restructured because, after all, the college needed money, students, and influence. The new rule was that thirty percent of the board members could be non-Zwinglians, but non-Zwinglians with money, of course. In view of changing convictions, the faculty determined that the mission statement of Christmas College should be revised to read: "The mission of Christmas College is to prepare students for effective citizenship by providing an education of quality in a caring community."

Then came the 1980s, and Christmas College boomed back. Enrollment climbed to more than three thousand, the science faculty was one of the strongest in the state, and the pre-med program was outstanding. A graduate received a Rhodes scholarship, and that was just one of many honors accorded to Christmas College graduates. There was a big capital campaign, and it succeeded in garnering plenty of non-Zwinglian money. The faculty expanded in numbers and quality, thus further enhancing the college's reputation for academic excellence. The truth be known, Christmas College was now a quite thoroughly secular institution: Chapel was held once a week and few attended, only one course in religion was required and that was in world religions, Zwinglian students were few in number, and there was only one Zwinglian professor left in the religion department and only a handful of Zwinglians on the faculty. Indeed, not even the president was a Zwinglian. The new requirement for membership on the Christmas College board of regents was that at least a third should be members of, or married to someone of, the Zwinglian denomination. The name of Christmas College started to seem a little quaint, out of step even with the mainstream. The year 1985 turned out to be a watershed for Christmas College when the name was changed with nearly unanimous support to Holiday College—a thoroughly inclusive title.

That moves us to the 1990s. Holiday College began preparations for its centennial. Someone wrote a history and discovered all those Zwinglians, which led to the reconsideration of some fundamental questions. This reconsideration had two dimensions, one intellectual and the other pragmatic. In the first instance, multiculturalism was sweeping the land and so the faculty, wanting to be up-to-date, said "Let's find out who we are," which meant, "Who were those Zwinglians?" There was a major capital campaign to go with the centennial celebration, which explains the pragmatic dimension of the reconsideration of basic issues. Many of the remnant Zwinglians had become very influential in central Iowa and beyond and, in the multicultural spirit of the age, they said "If you want us, you have to prove to us that you still honor us and our heritage." The non-Zwinglian faculty, a little defensive but not unresponsive, said, "But how do we deal with matters of Christian identity, much less Zwinglian identity. No one taught us how to do that in graduate school. In fact they taught us that religion was irrational, bah humbug stuff!" Others said, "When we were hired, that was not part of the bargain." But with the participation of a few highly-respected Zwinglians still in residence, the faculty began a quest for its identity and the alumni joined in too. Out of this came a major task force report, then a series of faculty workshops. A faculty study project sought to recover the distinctive themes of the Zwinglian tradition and then relate them to the intellectual and social life of the campus. Then a series of disciplinary-based study groups was formed. All agreed that as a consequence of these efforts the intellectual life of the college was revitalized, a sense of community was revived, and an emerging vision was unifying the campus. At their first meeting in 2000 the faculty adopted a new mission statement that reads, "The purpose of Holiday College is to prepare graduates for service in the world in a liberal arts context which is shaped by the Zwinglian tradition." Finally, some felt that perhaps the name, Holiday College, did not describe the place very well and that something more descriptive might be in order.

This fable of Christmas College mirrors the stories of church colleges told today by such reflective scholars as James Burtchaell, George Marsden, and Mark Noll. While the road to confusion about identity and mission and constituents traveled by Christmas College does not square with the story of every Lutheran college, neither are Lutheran colleges an exception to these tendencies. Indeed, for any culture-affirming institution that lives in a dialectical relationship with a pluralistic society, risks of these kinds are part of the enterprise.

What has this fable to do with the next decade and the next half-century? Will Lutheran colleges not be shaped by the national (or regional or global) economy, the public policies of state and nation, and competitive forces in both the academic marketplace and the real world? Of course, and Lutheran colleges dare not stint in their attention to such matters. Based on the record, they will not. While these material considerations are crucial to the future, I submit that the future of Lutheran colleges and universities will be even more profoundly shaped by the values, convictions, and traditions to which they choose to attend, and these matters, taken together, will shape the soul of Lutheran colleges.

For Lutheran colleges, it is always *kairos* time, time for decisions —incremental or climactic—that will profoundly shape the life of these colleges, the life of the church and society. Several scholars make the point that we are well into a post-Christian era when secular reality sets the agenda. In such times, people and institutions of faith are in the role of resident aliens, marching to a different drummer, working off a unique agenda, and often on the defensive. Some say all of that makes this a time of incredible opportunity for people and institutions of faith. There is some evidence for this. Consider the role of religion in the geopolitics of the world and in the dynamics of welfare reform and healthcare. Or notice the eagerness of increasing numbers of business people, professionals, parents, and scientists for conversation about values and ethics. Think about college students, seemingly unreconstructed materialists on the one hand, but putting in record hours of community service on the other and easily acknowledging the spiritual dimension in their lives. Perhaps this explains in part Francis Fukuyama's argument that religion is a significant force in re-moralizing America, and Steven Carter's view that a reformation of values is already underway.

Let's get closer to the challenge at the doorstep of a Lutheran college. While we have large numbers of students who are sensitive to their spirituality and the needs of their neighbors, the danger is that all of this is superficial. In the words of Bryan Hehir, a Roman Catholic and dean of Harvard Divinity School, what is needed is intellectual construction that will wed spirituality and generosity to personal existence and public life. Or if you prefer a Lutheran reading, consider the view of Valparaiso professor Richard Lee who describes ours as a post-intellectual society, awash in information if not reason: "It is a fraying democracy where the majority does not vote, fewer read, fewer discuss, and fewer care as education dumbs down, culture stupefies, and all that entertains is true." His encouraging word, addressed to Valparaiso grads and equally applicable to students at other Lutheran places, is this: "Happily, to that weighty, yet delicate task, many of you bring the ballast of the Christian intellectual tradition. Most of you can steady your intellectual life without wandering off into idols and ideologies, fads and fashion. To your intellectual life, you bring special understanding of the human condition, a view of the self and history, and finally a providence which transcends all that you may think and do, which can save you from both sentimentality and despair."

In my reading, these words are both evocative and reflective of the history, traditions, and convictions that are embedded in Lutheran colleges and that make a continuing claim upon the souls of these colleges and each of us who claim affiliation with these places. But how do we unpack the soul of a college? Is it possible to gain any precision in the face of something as abstract and ambiguous as soul talk? I believe it is possible to identify some of the elements which give life to the soul of a college, recognizing that the way in which those elements work together is a thing of mystery and, in our parlance, miracle; it is a process of both mind and Spirit with a capital "S." I will argue that the soul of a Lutheran college is shaped by the ways in which we respond to questions about epistemology, pedagogy, community, liturgy, and ecclesiology.

Epistemology

We begin to shape the soul of a Lutheran college by the way in which we respond to the question: How do we know and, by extension, what do we know and how shall we ascertain truth? These are epistemological matters. It is, as we shall see, the question that is back at the center of the intellectual forum following a long period of neglect. Now, you may say, undergraduate colleges are not principally about research or the discovery of truth. But the fact is that increasing numbers of our faculty members are engaged in expanding the frontiers of knowledge and, increasingly, they are engaging their students in such truth-seeking activities as well. Furthermore, teachers are unable to do justice to a field of inquiry without exploring its presuppositions, an exploration that inevitably leads to epistemological considerations.

For the person of faith, the search for truth is framed by certain convictions about the world and about scholarship. Consider the view of Father Michael S. Buckley, S.J., who wrote:

> Any academic movement towards meaning or coherence or truth, whether in the humanities, the sciences, or the professions, is inchoatively religious. This provocative statement obviously does not mean that qualitative mechanics or geography is religion or theology. It does mean that the intellectual dynamism inherent in all inquiry initiates processes or habits of questioning that—if not inhibited—invariably bear upon the ultimate questions that engage religion.

Ultimately, Buckley's convictions about scholarship and our convictions about life are not based on knowledge but on belief. As Peter L. Berger has written recently, Protestantism, with its "*sola fide* not only accepts the fact of uncertainty, but affirms that it is good." As George Marsden's analysis made clear, this Protestant view was held with great confidence and shaped, almost without question, the structure and content of American higher education in this country's first century. In his epic, *The Soul of the American University*, various social, economic, religious, and intellectual currents led to the erosion of religiously-based claims and the ascendancy of a scientific worldview. Hallmarks of this worldview are objectivity, pragmatism, naturalism, and optimism. It led human beings to believe that they were masters of the universe who could somehow do it all. In American higher education all of this led to the dominion of science over religion, of the naturalistic over the supernatural, of the technical and pragmatic over the humane and the spiritual.

This intellectual mindset began breaking down in the 1980s, damaged by the growing social chaos of religious wars, political exploitation, and economic inequality, and by such technical and scientific anomalies as the Challenger explosion and the AIDS epidemic. Scientific determinism was vulnerable to the thinking of people like Parker Palmer who argued for the interdependence of all things, material and spiritual; to scientists like William Pollard, who recognized the limits of material categories; to process theologians like John Cobb and Daniel Day Williams; and then to scores of post-modernists who saw the scientific enterprise as a perspective flawed by the ultimate human tendencies toward self-justification.

While all of this created a more hospitable environment for humanists in general and religious thought in particular, it is no sure thing. For one thing, the relativism of postmodernism is often based on naturalistic assumptions and tends toward nihilism, thus setting it at odds with Christian assumptions about the nature and purpose of existence. For another, Christian worldview advocates have been disabled and marginalized for so long by the scientific *zeitgeist* in the first instance and postmodernism in the second. Most of us come to the question of truth out of the convictions of faith. But, by and large, we had little opportunity or experience in relating those convictions to the real world search for truth in the academy, the public forum, or the marketplace. That is the result of a long period of marginalization and, given the academic venues of our graduate and professional training, that is not surprising. As a legion of contemporary writers such as Marsden, Sloan, and Noll make clear, colleges of the church have been handicapped as well. As Marsden puts it: "Many academics have deep moral and political convictions. What they most typically lack is the ability to provide a compelling intellectual rationale for these beliefs consistent with their other intellectual commitments." He goes on to argue that "liberal arts colleges with both strong religious identities and some openness to the larger academic community are in the best position to encourage serious Christian academic discourse." He encourages "vigorous programs to promote reflection on the implications of Christian perspectives," thus bringing the *sola fide* into the intellectual forum where truth is the shared objective. Marsden sees "most Christian perspectives as standing in paradoxical tension with mainstream academic ideals, not as Christianizing the mainstream."

The renaissance that is occurring on many church college campuses today is positive evidence in response to Marsden's challenge. This renaissance is being led by Reformed and Roman Catholic scholars in part, I suggest, because unlike Lutherans, they were not encumbered by our two kingdom mentality. But that situation is now changing with the recent work of Schwehn, Benne, and Simmons, and the vitality of such recent ventures as the Valparaiso-based Lilly Fellows Program, the Lutheran Academy of Scholars (ELCA), the Luther Institute Research Fellows, and the annual ELCA-sponsored Conference on the Vocation of a Lutheran College. On nearly a score of Lutheran campuses study around these issues is thriving and—make no mistake about it—this is soul work, *sola fide*! As inheritors and practitioners of a confessional, theological tradition, Lutherans have much to bring to the table. Consider, for example, the implications of the Lutheran understanding of Law and Gospel, the doctrine of the incarnation, Luther's convictions about our simultaneous existence as saint and sinner, the doctrine of vocation, and the world view implications of our creed. I submit that when such *sola fide* is engaged with real world search for truth, then we are doing "soul work."

Pedagogy

We do soul work in the pedagogical tasks that are central to our work as architects of our curricula, teachers of our texts, and mentors to our students. Let me focus on two significant pedagogical practices: the liberal arts and the dialectic between faith and learning. The liberal arts have been at the center of the way Lutherans think about and practice education from the beginning. What could be more appropriate for those who would practice Christian freedom than an educational pedagogy that focuses on the arts of leadership and service, freedom and responsibility? What could be more appropriate for people of faith who believe that "all things hold together" than an education that explores the various expressions of being human and the several dimensions of creation? The liberal arts are necessarily dynamic so we evaluate and reconsider our understanding and practice of these arts from time to time, but they remain at the soul of a Lutheran college.

Dialectic is the Lutheran mode, given life by Martin Luther and refined analysis by H. Richard Niebuhr. So for Lutheran colleges, talk of faith and learning is congenital in its origin. I hasten to say that it has perhaps never been a more challenging task than it is today. In the words of David Hollenbach of Boston College:

> Linking faith and culture is a more arduous undertaking today than ever before, precisely because of the complexity and diversity of contemporary academic disciplines and because of the deep pluralism of global culture. Only a protracted and sustained process of inquiry will make the effort to link faith and culture even partially successful. For this, intellectual as well as moral fortitude will be needed.

And, the Lutheran scholar would add, a healthy dose of skepticism is also necessary on account of the human tendency to rationalize evil on the one hand and faith and revelation on the other. So this soul claim of our heritage is not to be taken lightly. Responsibility for dialectical pedagogy of the sort we have inherited will not be adequately nurtured with an occasional workshop or brown-bag seminar. It requires constant attention and rigorous scholarship. Clearly, it is not for the faint of heart or the mere enthusiast.

Community

The soul work of a Lutheran college is also carried out in the life of the community. This conviction is grounded in our understanding of the third article of our creed, which speaks of community in Christ. Ronald Thiemann has written about the importance of grounding our intellectual task in community. He wrote:

> Only those public intellectuals who are genuine, connected critics, people connected to real flesh-and-blood communities of commitment and engagement, can provide guidance for those of us who struggle to be

faithful to our spiritual commitments in a complex and changing world.

Lutheran places will differ from secular academic communities because they see colleagues and students as children of God called to *agape* love for the neighbor. Seeing staff, students, teachers, and constituents as members of one body, differing in roles, interdependent in function, and united in spirit is an entirely different image than that of a community defined merely by shared geography, procedures, expectations, and codes of conduct. For Lutheran colleges, the communitarian ethic has a specific locus in the biblical and confessional traditions. These traditions give Lutheran colleges a unique frame of reference in proclaiming and being communities. It means that these institutions lean against the wind of expressive individualism and utilitarianism, to borrow from the Bellah group's work. It means that Lutheran places are attentive to both the welfare of each person and the health of the whole, a balancing act too often out of balance. It means that they are concerned about virtue, about compassion and justice, not for the sake of their annual crime reports but for the sake of soul.

Liturgy

For Lutheran colleges the question of community is virtually inseparable from the question of liturgy. I take some license here by applying the term to a range of community events from worship to celebration, from the arts to athletics, from convocations to the rituals of homecomings. It is a long time since Peter Berger wrote his influential work, *The Sacred Canopy*. In it he argued that institutions have a "plausibility structure." That is, they stand for something and they are plausible, they are viable, to the degree that that "something" is kept alive in the hearts, lives, and souls of the members. Now the something that defines the plausibility of Lutheran colleges is found in their mission, expressed in their culture, and embodied in their faculty and students, both collectively and individually. And it is kept alive in a variety of liturgies. From all we know about matters of spirit and mind, those liturgical acts are absolutely essential to the plausibility of these colleges. Indeed, one writer, James W. Lewis, elevates the role of liturgy in the soul shaping of an institution:

Though Christianity is a serious intellectual matter, it is also a way of living one's life, immersed in a rich complex of symbols, practices, and rituals. On the college campus the latter may be Christianity's most important contribution and its greatest opportunity (*Christian Century*, May 19-26, 1999, page 577).

Think about worship for a minute. We believe that when the community is gathered and the Word is proclaimed and the sacraments are shared, something miraculous occurs. We are shaped by the experience because the Spirit of God is present. Again, Thiemann makes the connection between worship and the intellectual task:

> By engaging in prayer and righteous action, our communities of faith can provide the indispensable context within which true public intellectuals might be nurtured. Through acts of worship, education, and service we witness to our hope that the whole of God's creation 'will be set free from its bondage to decay and [will] obtain the glorious liberty of the children of God.

Given this assumption, it is simply impossible to over-estimate the impact of worship in the life of a Lutheran college. It nurtures the soul, individually and collectively. But the tragedy of it is, worship is a neglected treasure on most campuses. Whether due to busyness or individualism, daily worship tends to be marginalized in most schedules, and so the Holy Spirit is not overworked but overlooked. I do not know what the long-term price of such neglect will be, but we should not underestimate it.

Turn next to the liturgical act of making music. We are heirs of Luther who said that after theology, music has the "highest place and the greatest honor." He also said: "Experience proves that next to the word of God only music deserves to be extolled as the mistress and governess of the feelings of the human heart." Reflect on the influence of the Christmas concerts held annually at most Lutheran colleges. In many cases, more than half the students are involved in making music, painting sets, running lights and sound, preparing food, or parking cars. Whether Lutheran or Buddhist or unbeliever, there is a witness. Years later the words of the Messiah may come alive in the new and unexpected circumstances of a family wedding, a class reunion, or a personal crisis. Such liturgical events define the "ultimate concerns" of such places.

Yes, and so too do convocations and commencements. They denote the serious business of an academic institution's call to glorify God by doing the best academic work of which the community is capable. Football games and homecoming dances all reflect devotion to each other and the capacity to rejoice in our common humanity. Yes, the liturgy of common life is powerful, at once a thing of grace and a mode of creation. These liturgical acts make a unique contribution to the plausibility of a Lutheran college; they are soul food for a holy people.

Ecclesiastical Relationships

Finally, the soul of a Lutheran college will be shaped by ecclesiastical relationships. By ecclesiastical, I refer to the college's relationship to the church. Lutheran colleges were born in the heart of the church. Through most of history, the churchly sponsorship of Lutheran colleges has determined the mission, provided the students, shaped the curriculum and credo, and somehow produced the financial wherewithal to keep these places alive. The colleges were a central priority of the church, and the church in turn was a central priority for the colleges. This confessional and experiential focus led many colleges to see themselves as colleges of the church. While church and congregation had unique callings, they saw themselves as members of the same body, united in spirit and mission.

Now a good deal has changed, particularly in the past fifty years. Pluralism and secularism have changed the relationship equation. The church has new challenges and, in the inevitable realignment of priorities, church colleges have been moved to the periphery. On the basis of recent research by Hartwick-Day, we know that graduates of Lutheran colleges are having a significant impact on the church, and their educational experiences are qualitatively different from the education provided in the public sector. Those differences reflect both the religious and humane commitments of Lutheran colleges. We may hope that as these data are more widely shared, the church and its constituent elements will draw closer to the colleges. But as things now stand, the relationship of the church to its colleges is not regulatory but permissive, not obligatory but voluntary, not central but peripheral. Not surprisingly, this has led some colleges to distance themselves from the ecclesiastical dimension of their existence.

I hope and trust that most Lutheran colleges will continue to answer the ecclesiastical question in an affirmative way. To do so would be consistent with their history and a rich confessional understanding. In doing so they will honor and keep alive a relationship that nurtures them spiritually and intellectually. In their first century or more, Lutheran colleges in America needed the church for both their material and spiritual well being. I submit that today the church needs colleges (perhaps more than it realizes) for the reasons Richard Lee noted when he said that graduates of places like these bring to the culture and, I might add, the church "the ballast of the Christian intellectual tradition" along with passion for community, justice, and service.

Conclusion

I have saved my most important thesis until now as a way of underscoring its importance. My transcending thesis is that the soul of Lutheran colleges will come alive in and through its people, and the people most central to this are the faculty and staff. Their understanding of the mission and tradition of the college will matter more than the rhetoric of the catalog, the commitments of the external constituents, or the transient values of the students. It is, therefore, essential that faculty and staff be well qualified and well fed, both materially and spiritually, both academically and theologically, for on this element more than any other hangs the future and the soul of Lutheran colleges. To be sure, their future will reflect the economy and the culture and the political climate. But the fundamental compass for a Lutheran college will be its soul. *Sola fide. Soli Deo Gloria.*

Works Cited

Peter Berger, "Protestantism and the Quest for Certainty," *Christian Century*, August 26–September 2, 1998.

Michael S. Buckley, SJ, *The Catholic University as Promise and Project* (Washington, D.C.: Georgetown University Press, 1998).

John P. Langan, SJ, editor, *Catholic Universities in Church and Society; a Dialogue on Ex Corde Ecclesia* (Washington, D.C.: Georgetown University Press, 1993).

Richard Lee in *Context*, April 15, 1998.

James W. Lewis review in *Christian Century*, May 19-26, 1999.

George Marsden letter in *Christian Century*, June 16-23, 1999.

George Marsden, *The Outrageous Idea of Christian Scholarship* (New York: Oxford University Press, 1997).

George Marsden, *The Soul of the American University: From Protestant Establishment to Established Unbelief* (New York: Oxford University Press, 1994).

Douglas Sloan, *Faith and Knowledge: Mainline Protestantism and American Higher Education* (Louisville, Kentucky: Westminster John Knox Press, 1994).

Ronald Thiemann, *Religion and Values in Public Life*, Fall, 2000.

CHAPTER NINE

Lutheran Higher Education in a Postmodern, Post-Christian Era

Lutheran Educational Conference of North America
February 5, 2001

Following my retirement from Concordia in 1999, I spent a term as a visiting scholar at the Kennedy School of Harvard University. The focus of my research was the future of religious colleges in a postmodern world. This led to a national conference on the subject and an edited selection of the papers presented at the event. This was an unprecedented opportunity for me to study the relevant issues and develop some perspective on where all of the intellectual and social tumult of the 1990s might be leading Lutheran colleges and universities. So I responded with alacrity when invited to address the Lutheran Educational Conference of North America. As you will see, I was both sanguine about the challenges and optimistic about the prospects for Lutheran colleges that mined and minded their unique resources.

The November 2000 issue of *The Lutheran* included the annual feature on Lutheran higher education. There were mini-features published describing noteworthy achievements and anecdotes about students who excel in a variety of ways. But the title of the feature essay was "Still Lutheran?" and the lead sentences were these: "Are Lutheran colleges and universities abandoning their roots in the Lutheran tradition? It is a concern that administrators grapple with constantly as they try to balance the unique missions of their institutions with the demands of society and the marketplace."

While I might have wished for a different title and lead line, we all may concede the validity of the underlying question. That question has been a centerpiece of many of the recent meetings of Lutheran

Educational Conference of North America (LECNA); few among us have not been planting and nurturing discussion of these issues on our campuses.

What is true for Lutherans is true for our sisters and brothers across the denominational spectrum, which explains the rationale for the 2000 Harvard conference on "The Future of Religious Colleges." This gathering of seventeen presenters and eighty participants represented a broad spectrum of religious denominations from evangelical and Pentecostal to mainline and confessional.

I will respond to my assignment by reporting on the major themes of the Harvard conference, and I will bring implications from the conference to bear on the question: What is the future of Lutheran higher education in a postmodern, post-Christian era?

The Harvard Conference

A student of religious higher education could describe the last decade of the twentieth century as a time of revitalization. As evaluators of the Lilly Endowment's *Initiative on Religion and Higher Education* concluded, "There is today more discussion about the role of religion in the academy than at any time in the past forty years and more commitment to the project of Christian higher education than there was just ten years ago." The staging for this renewal was formed by a convergence of now familiar events during the preceding decades. First, there were changes in the identity and self-understanding of many religious colleges. Whether by neglect or design, the relationship of many colleges to their mainstream denominational sponsors changed or diminished. Another informing event was the secularization of the society and its institutions in a post-Constantinian, postmodern, post-religious time. Another development was the marginalized status of religiously informed scholarship in the academy. And finally, public policy at both local and federal levels shaped the context in which religious colleges pursued their work.

In consequence of these developments, most of these colleges became more religiously diverse in the composition of their faculties, staffs, and student bodies, and more secular in character and content. From a material point of view, most of them prospered, from an academic point of view most improved, and from a cultural perspective, the graduates of these institutions exercised a positive impact. But the crisis of religious identity was widely experienced among religious institutions across nearly all faith perspectives.

Such abstract markers as these do not begin to provide the yeast for the revitalization that is now under way. Human agents and agencies with names, agendas, and histories of their own provided that yeast. One thinks of the work of such public intellectuals as Glen Tinder, Stephen Carter, Robert Putnam, Robert Bellah, and Alisdair MacIntyre. In a series of widely acclaimed books and essays, Tinder and Carter voiced concern for the marginalization of religious belief in our public life; Putnam and Bellah raised the level of awareness about the growth of individualism and the disengagement of citizens from civic responsibility; and MacIntyre illuminated the role of tradition-based communal practices in shaping the moral character of a people.

While these issues were being given voice in the public square, others were raising a related set of issues in the academic square. Landmark work includes George Marsden's assessment of the soul of the American university; Douglas Sloan's comprehensive analysis of the plight of religiously informed scholarship; Mark Noll's assessment of the evangelical academic project; James Burtchaell's dour and provocative analysis of the social history of a diverse set of religious colleges; and the Lilly Endowment-sponsored examination of the diverse stories and traditions of religious colleges. Add to this work the quakes and aftershocks of denominational actions affecting Roman Catholic and Baptist institutions, the vitality of the evangelical colleges, and both the fair and foul winds of public policy, and you begin to measure the dimensions of a watershed time for religious higher education.

Most of the seminal scholarship undergirding the current revitalization is critical and historical in method and character. The burden of the Harvard Conference was to project the future, an assignment that most scholars prefer to avoid. But hearty and resourceful band that they are, the scholars who joined us in Cambridge gave it their best. The conference was organized around five central questions.

The first of these inquired about the future of religiously informed scholarship. This is, in a sense, the epistemological question and it speaks to the viability of religious scholarship in a postmodern age. George Marsden has blazed the trail on this issue over the past decade. He rehearsed for us his analysis of the rise and fall of what he calls "progressive scientific humanism," a mindset that held sway for the first six decades of the twentieth century and argued that, "humankind was progressing largely due to scientific advance." As a result, religiously informed scholarship was marginalized and the arts and humanities were diminished. Marsden then made his argument about the collapse of this epistemology, a collapse evident in the demise of the Soviet empire and in the loss of confidence in the promise of the progressive scientific idea. Marsden did not suggest the abandonment of the scientific method by any means, only the scientific ideology. Marsden went on, in an autobiographical way, to illustrate how religious scholarship can be both religiously substantive and academically viable. A subsequent presenter, Joel Carpenter of Calvin College, added the weight of his own evidence to Marsden's argument by noting the emergence of a growing cadre of respected religious scholars in recent decades, many of whom are products of Dutch Reformed colleges.

Douglas Sloan of Columbia Teachers College was not as optimistic about the viability of religious scholarship. His now landmark analysis of the failed struggles of religious scholars in the twentieth century is compelling. In his estimation, the church adopted the modern conception of knowledge and thus cut the ground out from its own pre-suppositions. "What is required" for a fruitful engagement of faith and knowledge, said Sloan, "is a radical transformation of our ways of knowing, such that qualitative ways of knowing lay claim to no less rigor, cogency, and necessity than the quantitative." In a subsequent paper, Mark Noll of Wheaton College argued that, with respect to the Christian parts of the fuller picture, we are not experiencing a renaissance of Christian intellectual life. Both Sloan and later Mark Schwehn argue that any renaissance is made difficult in the modern academy that is shaped internally by the reigning reward system and externally by powerful and global material interests. But on balance, in these presentations and subsequent discussion, one senses a growing confidence about the vitality and credibility of Christian scholars in the academy.

The second set of papers spoke to the question: Is the trend toward disengagement from a distinctive religious identity and mission inevitable? Or, to put it in the vernacular, is there really a "slippery slope?" James Burtchaell, while not a presenter, was perhaps the most quoted source at the conference—a tribute to his ability to make an argument and stimulate good dialogue. The Reverend David M. O'Connell, president of Catholic University, argued that disengagement is not inevitable and set out some preconditions for strong and continuing engagement. Those preconditions are that there is an institutional imperative to remain religious and, second, that the religious identity of the college is evident in the operations and activities of the college. Mark Noll, on the other hand, argued that the narrative of decline is most characteristic in the historiography of religious colleges. While he does not see a renaissance in Christian intellectual life, he does believe there is more and better self-consciously Christian learning going on than in any previous era in our history since the seventeenth century. Alan Wolfe's *Atlantic Monthly* essay on evangelical colleges appeared on the eve of the conference and provided additional data in support of Noll's view. Philip Gleason, the distinguished historian of Catholic higher education, weighed in with his view that *Ex Corde Ecclesia* is an effort to reverse the trend toward disengagement. Michael Beaty of Baylor University described initiatives among several Baptist colleges, including his own, as efforts to redefine, but not disengage from, relationship to the church.

These papers about disengagement were integral to the third major inquiry of the conference: Can colleges that have lost their church-relatedness be transformed? Or, if you prefer, can churches that have lost their college-relatedness be transformed? While Monika Hellwig of the American Association of Catholic Colleges and Universities sees *Ex Corde Ecclesia*, taken at its best, as an opportunity to strengthen the relationship between the Catholic Church and its colleges, other conference participants were reserved and even pessimistic about that possibility. Indeed, the working out of identity and relationship issues in Roman Catholic and Baptist higher education may be a portent for other religious colleges. We shall follow these developments with care and hope for the colleges, the church, and society.

Turning to other denominational sectors, we heard encouraging stories of constructive engagement between colleges and judicatories. In the Mennonite and Nazarene traditions there is an intimate and symbiotic relationship between colleges and church. Samuel DuBois Cook's account of the partnership of the United Methodist Church with its related Black colleges is a story of prophetic, servant-oriented leadership. Other mainstream Protestant stories are more ambiguous. Robert Benne and Mark Schwehn both wondered whether or not there are enough committed believers in the religious body—committed to the higher education venture, that is—to insure the college-relatedness of the church. Relationships are less secure in the mainline churches; the church-relatedness of colleges continues in decline, as does the college-relatedness of church bodies. This means that relationship and identity issues are housed primarily with the colleges, places caught in the maelstrom of competing interests and loyalties. Indeed, the times will test again whether or not relationship to a religious entity is essential to the faithfulness of a religious college. Again, as Burtchaell and others have chronicled it, the historical record is not encouraging.

Reformed and evangelical college institutions that provide the backbone of the membership of the Council of Christian Colleges and Universities have shown remarkable growth in financial strength, enrollment, and by many measures, quality, over the past decade. Joel Carpenter, in his aptly titled essay, "The Perils of Prosperity," wondered whether, as these colleges broaden their reach, they might lose their distinctiveness. Other spokespersons for this tradition were sanguine about issues in their experience, issues related to fundamentalism on the one hand and a growing self-conscious commitment to the broader international, pluralistic culture on the other. People from across the denominational spectrum wondered about the impact of declining denominationalism on the relationship between church and college.

The fourth cluster of papers addressed the question of whether and how the diverse educational missions of religious colleges might be sustained. This discussion was shaped by the Richard T. Hughes and William B. Andrian volume, *Models for Christian Higher Education.* Six writers addressed these questions by projecting their respective traditions into the future. It was a rich discussion. Philip Gleason, with credit to Notre Dame colleague Mark Roche, described the features of the Roman Catholic tradition. Joel Carpenter provided a lucid account of the Kyperian vision that shapes colleges in the Dutch

Reformed tradition. Judson Carlberg described the wonderfully coherent vision of the evangelical colleges and the tensions with which they deal. Samuel DuBois Cook spoke of the "intellectual love of God" and its implications for United Methodist higher education and the prophetic role of its Black colleges. Paul Keim of Goshen College shared with us the ways in which the Anabaptist tradition shapes life and learning at Mennonite colleges. Mark Schwehn, whose reputation for thoughtfulness is well known to this group, predicted that the future of Lutheran identity might be shaped around the response to four key issues:

> First, to what extent, if any, can universities credibly remain integral and coherent communities of learning without transcendent horizons? Second, can the higher learning in America retain its vitality if it loses the plurality of institutions that collectively advance it? Third, can the persistent decline of liberal learning relative to so-called vocational preparation be arrested without some kind of imaginative re-conception of the whole relationship between liberal education and vocational training? Finally, a question that in some ways encompasses all of the others: Can a liberal democracy continue to be served by a higher education that exalts ideas of freedom, enlightenment, progressive development, problem-solving, and the relief of humankind's estate without commensurate attention to the meaning and significance of the overwhelming facts of human mortality and finitude?

We also took account of Alan Wolfe's question about whether or not evangelical colleges can manage the critical edge that he deems prerequisite to the sort of intellectual engagement to which these colleges aspire. As some described and critiqued their respective traditions, others saw their own tradition in a new light. In this way, we demonstrated our conviction that it is not capitulation to relativism to say that we respect our differences unless we cease to care about those differences.

The fifth and final shaping inquiry was stated thusly: Will public policy and the interpretation thereof be an ally or an enemy of religious colleges? Public policy and, in particular, constitutional law at both state and federal levels is not benign, though as Kent Weeks argued, the current milieu is rather favorable to distinctively religious colleges. But is it possible that a differently constituted Supreme Court could revisit the Tilton or Roemer decisions? Could the concern on the left for federal funding of faith-based services raise similar concerns about faith-based educational ventures? My own concerns run more in the direction of state venues. We find a wide range of law and precedent among the states. For example, some states permit institutions to require faith statements from employees while others do not. Might secularists in other states draw encouragement from a case currently pending in Washington State that challenges the eligibility of students attending religious colleges to receive state grants? Some Roman Catholics wonder whether or not the mandates of *Ex Corde Ecclesia* will place institutions of that church body in conflict with civil rights and/or human rights legislation in some states. It seems safe to say that in our increasingly litigious society we will need to be attentive to these issues in order to maintain a climate as positive as the one that we now enjoy.

While these comments summarize responses to the five inquires identified at the outset, new areas of inquiry emerged in the course of the conference. There is the issue of the ecology of campus communities, the question of the connections between teaching and scholarship, and the matter of the distinction between vocation and vocationalism. Both the questions we visited and the ones that we discovered will provide grist for new and continuing inquiry.

Now let me undertake a second summary, namely to characterize the dialogue of this event. The first characteristic that comes to mine is variety—variety in the ways traditions think of identity and mission, variety in the ways in which they relate to their sponsoring religious bodies, variety in their histories, and variety in the constituencies they serve and the expectations of those constituencies. For example, most of the evangelical and Roman Catholic institutions are homogenous in the composition of faculty and staff, while the mainline Protestant colleges are less so. Some institutions have an intentional openness and engagement with our worldly culture, while others are more decidedly focused on their own traditions and vision.

In a pluralistic world, religious colleges both reflect the mosaic and contribute to it, each trying to walk the tightrope between distinctiveness and engagement. Because our stories are so unique, options about the future will necessarily be highly individualized as well.

Another subtext in the discussion was the resourcefulness and the vigor of these institutions. There is a resourcefulness about religious colleges that is remarkable. Issues of identity and relationship are on the table, relationships are being reconsidered and recast, and more attention is being given to the intellectual task of religious colleges and religiously informed scholarship than at any time in at least the last half century. Amidst the company of institutions represented at the conference, one sees program innovation, enrollment growth, and collaborative ventures of many kinds—all of which proves again the resourcefulness of these colleges and their important place in the future of American higher education. A transcending theme in these papers and proceedings was a clearly distinguishable mood of hopefulness. The energy of the conference also reflected a broader dynamic in the land. Religiously-informed scholarship is finding an expanding audience, initiatives to revisit and reshape issues of identity and mission are widespread among us, and faculty development initiatives around the themes of this conference are well-supported and well-received. As Baptist institutions reconfigure their relationships to the church, they do so out of a sense of possibility; the Nazarene colleges relate to those they serve with an exciting vision; and, in most cases, Roman Catholic institutions appear to approach the implementation of *Ex Corde Ecclesia* from a position of strength. As Lutherans pursue new modes of self-examination and theological formation, one senses an emerging vitality with their traditions as well.

But we Lutherans do, as you know, both bless and curse reason, for we are confirmed dialecticians. So we read the signs and envision our future with a sense of contingency, a mood that, we discover, is shared by others. How do we find our way in a society that shapes education around utilitarian needs and in an academy in which community building is an increasingly lost art? How do we maintain or in many cases reconstruct relationships between colleges and judicatories? Using Mark Schwehn's language, how do we construct a transcending vision and an awareness of the realities of death and human mortality in a culture of consumption, control, and immediacy? Or again, to what extent will religiously-informed scholarship be viable in an academy shaped by scientific determinism and/or postmodern fatalism? So we see through a glass darkly, but we do see because we are looking. We are looking because there is something in our souls that is in a quest for meaning and significance, a quest that is shaped by a transcending vision and the certainty of an ineffable grace.

Thus far, my rendering of the Harvard conference serves, in large measure, as context for what I offer in response to the second controlling question in this presentation: What is the future of Lutheran higher education in a postmodern, post-Christian era? Once again, let me organize my response around five constituent questions.

The first of which is this: How shall we culture-friendly, two-kingdom thinking Lutherans live in the world without conforming to the world? The Thomist and neo-Thomist Roman Catholics and our Kyperian Reformed and evangelical colleagues possess an intellectual credo that shaped scholarship and academic life in fairly straightforward ways. But, while finding strength in our confessional and ethnic traditions, Lutherans were not well served by our dualistic inducing two kingdoms theology. In the tradition of Luther, Melanchthon, and Bach, we affirm the world, or culture if you will, as a place of God's continuing creation. And while Luther insisted that the two kingdoms were dimensions of a single reality, the two kingdoms formulation was easily misread and perhaps led us into a preoccupation with first article, earthly kingdom issues. The advent of what Marsden calls "progressive scientific humanism" has exacerbated the problem for Lutherans.

So is there hope for us? Well, yes, both in our tradition and in these postmodern times. The doctrine of the incarnation is a corrective to misguided understandings of the two kingdoms. In the words of Paul, all things hold together in Christ, "all things in heaven and on earth." Recall that our confessional tradition consists of three articles, not one. It affirms the interconnections between and among Creator, Redeemer, and Holy Spirit on the one hand and between and among creation, creatures, and community on the other. Indeed, in our confessions and theology we discern consistently a pattern of engagement and a quest for wholeness.

I believe that in postmodern times Lutherans have a unique gift to bring to the academic circle in our understanding of dialectic, our sense of contingency, our inclination toward the paradoxical, our understanding of the virtues and the limits of human reason, and our approach to issues of vocation. I submit that these are significant gifts in a postmodern time, a time that underscores the paradoxical nature of reality, the often decisive influence of context, the contingency of human knowledge, and the role of community in defining truth. As Lutherans we can identify with such uncertainties as these, for we have always known about them. But we are not circumscribed by them, for we know the one who is Truth, we know the one who ultimately reconciles that which is seemingly irreconcilable, we know the one who creates community and provides the grace to transcend human contingencies. So yes, Lutherans have the tools to live in the world without conforming to the world. This postmodern time is a time to rethink old things; it is a new opening for disciples as fundamental issues of meaning and truth are on the table.

Question two: How shall we preserve and enrich the confessional tradition that undergirds our identity as Lutheran colleges? I think the answers here are fairly obvious. They are embodied in projects underway in our church bodies and on most of our campuses, projects to nurture our leaders, our teachers, and our staff members. As I noted at the outset, in the annual programs of this conference we have found nurture in the scholarship of Mark Schwehn, Richard T. Hughes, Martin Marty, Richard John Neuhaus, Ernest Simmons, and others. In the ELCA, which I know best, the annual conference on "The Vocation of a Lutheran College" has met with enthusiasm and served as an impetus for a variety of campus-based programs.

In addition, it is absolutely vital that we nurture our intellectuals. Until recent days, the primary intellectual leadership in the current renaissance came out of the Roman Catholic or Dutch Reformed traditions. Then Lutherans Mark Schwehn and Robert Benne entered the conversation and, more recently, Ernest Simmons, De Ane Lagerquist, and others. While we are somewhat late comers, the hallway conversations during the Harvard conference reflected both great respect for, and expectations of, Lutheran scholars. And, I submit, the people in this assembly will have a lot to do with that. Our scholars need to be recognized, encouraged, and supported. I believe the ELCA's new Lutheran Academy is a project with great potential and the Luther Institute's fellowship program is another. Among other things, they open the possibility of building a sustaining community of scholars who may be in service to church, colleges, and culture.

The embodiment of a Lutheran *logos* will require more than scholarship, however. It will also require a re-vitalized pedagogy. You think immediately as I do of an invigorated dialogue between faith and learning in our classrooms. In our postmodern age this kind of dialogue has become both permissible and desirable in an increasing number of academic venues.

The third question I raise for your consideration: So how may we develop and sustain this faith and learning dialogue? The Lilly Fellows Program provides a splendid opportunity on an inter-campus, ecumenical level. In addition, several Lutheran colleges are providing opportunities for faculty members to develop these skills that their graduate school mentors would have frowned upon. In their recently published evaluation of the Lilly initiatives, the authors suggest initiatives that facilitate campus-wide conversation that may lead to institutional change. They also recommend faculty development initiatives designed to cultivate a sense of vocation among graduate students and junior faculty. In addition, they recommend programs geared to faculty at various stages in their career trajectory.

When speaking of pedagogy, I want to expand the definition beyond the classroom to encourage worship and community. The subjectivism and individualism of postmodernity and the specialization and materialism of modernity are, to say the least, inhospitable to worship and community. Which of our campuses has not seen worship marginalized and community fractured in at least small ways? Yet both the confessions and praxis of our tradition underscore the essential integration of faith and worship, faith and community. I use the term figuratively when I say that we need to cultivate the pedagogies of worship and community and, while our tradition provides both motive and models for such activity, we will need to be inventive and enterprising if we are to break out of the conundrums most campuses experience today. Giving some focused reflection to these pedagogical imperatives would be a starting point.

The fourth question that speaks to the Lutheran future is this: How shall we strengthen our relationship with other members of the church body of which we are a part. When the Apostle Paul spoke of the body as a collection of interdependent and essential members, he was describing the church. Working out of that image, the health of church and its member parts, including our colleges and universities, are interdependent. The LECNA project to reclaim Lutheran students speaks to that interdependence in one way; the creative global mission activities that many colleges have initiated in consort with synods of the church is another; and a myriad of congregational service enterprises is yet another expression of this interdependence.

But the research phase of the "reclaiming" project indicated the distance we have to go in strengthening the relationship beyond the enrollment of students. Maybe we need to add other dimensions to the reclamation project. For example, what can we learn from some of our faith communities that are initiating practices of physical, social, and spiritual healing? What can we learn about hospitality from some of our church growth centers? What about building coalitions with health and human service ministries of the church? And can we form more constructive alliances with congregations around issues of education for vocation and leadership? How about launching new cooperative initiatives in response to the coming shortage of clergy in our churches? You may add your own initiatives to this list and, to be sure, we cannot do it without the cooperation of other members of the family. But perhaps the time has come to try some new strategies, for we live in a strange time of abundant resources but seemingly meager imagination and will.

Conclusion

Our postmodern, post-Christian future is characterized by change and complexity. The more complex our future, the more disciplined must be the church and its leaders. So what are the disciplines that will be required of college presidents in such an age? Surely study and reflection are first in line. By gathering around issues of identity and mission at these annual meetings and other related conferences, we are practicing these disciplines. By initiating and funding a variety of faculty and staff development initiatives, we are cultivating the essential human infrastructure on which the future of our colleges will be built. By taking the lead in the reclaiming project, we have made a commitment to the development of leaders for both college and church. These activities will continue to be paramount in defining and embodying Lutheran identity in a postmodern, post-Christian era. Given the circumstances facing our churches in this post-denominational time, the significant leadership burden in these matters will rest with you and our campus colleagues.

To this list of work, add some familiar elements to the agenda of identity enrichment. The development and selection of your successors will be absolutely critical. Every search for an academic dean or a president will underscore the challenge of identifying candidates formed in the tradition and poised to bring leadership to our institutions in this new era. The selection of board members will be crucial. If we have to soften our image to attract the people we think we need on our boards or regents, that is a problem, but probably more solvable in a postmodern time. Board development focused around mission is just as important as faculty development. Presidential minding of the faculty selection process to insure more than a critical mass of faculty who will embody and advocate for our mission will be critical and, again, may be easier to accomplish in a postmodern age when religious particularity is once more on the screen.

Each of our institutional contexts is unique. One formula will not fit all. Presidential leadership will continue to be crucial in these matters. We rejoice in such challenges because, if we look and listen closely, we will hear and see God's promise in the change. In Marva Dawn's words: "The postmodern world that surrounds us yearns for stability, morality, security, fidelity, faith, hope, and love. These deep needs can only be met through the one who meets our deepest need for truth." And there, I submit, is the promise.

Works Cited

James Tunstead Burtchaell, *The Dying of the Light: The Disengagement of Colleges and Universities from Their Christian Churches* (Grand Rapids: Wm. B. Eerdmans Publishing Co., 1998).

Marva Dawn, *Lutheran Partners*, (May/June 1998).

Philip Gleason, *Contending with Modernity: Catholic Higher Education in the 20th Century* (New York: Oxford University Press, 1996).

Richard Hughes and William B. Andrian, editors, *Models of Christian Higher Education: Strategies for Survival in the Twenty-First Century* (Grand Rapids: Wm. B. Eerdmans Pubishing Company, 1997).

Mark A. Noll, *The Scandal of the Evangelical Mind* (Grand Rapids: Wm. B. Eerdmans Pubishing Co., 1994).

Kathleen A. Mahoney, John Schmalzbauer & James Youniss, *Revitalizing Religion in the Academy*, (Chestnut Hill, Massachusetts: Boston College, 2000).

George M. Marsden, *The Soul of the American University: From Protestant Establishment to Established Unbelief* (New York: Oxford University Press, 1994).

George M. Marsden, *The Outrageous Idea of Christian Scholarship* (New York: Oxford University Press, 1997).

William C. Ringenberg, editor, *The Christian College: A History of Protestant Higher Education in America* (Grand Rapids: Wm. B. Eerdmans Pubishing Co., 1984).

Douglas Sloan, *Faith and Knowledge: Mainline Protestantism and American Higher Education* (Louisville, Kentucky: Westminster John Knox Press, 1994).

Alan Wolfe, "The Opening of the Evangelical Mind," *The Atlantic Monthly*, October 2000.

CHAPTER TEN

Lutheran Intellectuals and the Church

Lutheran College Dean's Meeting, Chicago, Illinois

In the fall of 2001, I was invited to address the annual meeting of the Lutheran college deans on the role of Lutheran intellectuals in the church. This was another opportunity to share what I had recently been reading, thinking, and writing with reference to postmodernism and religious colleges. It was also an opportunity to address some of the ways in which the church and its intellectuals might interact for their mutual edification.

This is an opportunity to address two questions: What can the church do to support the Lutheran intellectual tradition through its colleges and universities? And what can Lutheran intellectuals in our colleges and universities do in support of the church?

Before addressing these matters, please indulge me an autobiographical note. In 1978 I heard a lecture that profoundly shaped my vocation as a Lutheran educator. The speaker was David Lotz of Union Theological Seminary, and the title of his lecture was "Education for Citizenship in the Two Kingdoms: Reflections on the Theological Foundations of Lutheran Higher Education." He opened a glimpse for me of the Lutheran intellectual tradition that I had scarcely heard discussed up until that point in my academic career. I was, like most of you and many of our institutions, a product, and in some ways a victim, of the Enlightenment.

To move from past to present, I recently read Richard T. Hughes' excellent new book, *How Christian Faith Can Sustain the Life of the Mind.* He writes:

> The Lutheran tradition possesses some of the most potent theological resources for sustaining the life of the

mind that one could imagine. It encourages a dialogue between the Christian faith and the world of ideas, fosters intellectual humility, engenders a healthy suspicion of absolutes, and helps create a conversation in which all the conversation partners are taken seriously.

Then he raises a caution flag, saying that paradox is also our weakness. In nurturing both sides of a paradox it is easy to sacrifice one side for the other. In his words: "When the paradox dissolves in this way, the risks can be absolutism on the one hand, and relativism on the other." This tendency is especially apparent in considering the two kingdoms. If we accentuate the kingdom of God we are absolutizing our religious vision as the scholastics did. On the other hand, if we accentuate the secular, we run the risk of relativism. "Indeed, apart from its insistence on the kingdom of God, the Lutheran tradition would easily resemble a flaccid secular ideology in which nothing is ultimate, transcendent, or absolute."

I believe that the Lutheran commitment to secular scholarship combined with the slippery slope of our pedagogy of paradox made us especially susceptible to the epistemology of the Enlightenment. We bought into its values and that led us to eschew the non-rational and non-observable. Marsden documented the case, and I believe that Lutherans in some ways exemplified it for we were tempted to squeeze the religious, the spiritual, the emotional, and the aesthetic out of our enterprise or, alternatively, compartmentalized them. We came out the other side discovering that we had marginalized the heavenly kingdom in pursuit of the reining scholarly model.

Then about a decade ago, we became aware that we were losing our uniqueness as actively religious, Lutheran scholars and colleges. Much of what had sustained us—our worship, our sense of community, and a widely shared religious ethos—had grown weak. There were few powerful scholars in the Lutheran academy or the religious academy generally who could sustain the paradox of Christ and culture, faith and learning. As we began to ache for what we had lost and search for scholars who could give voice to our quest for renewal – the voices were most often Roman or Reformed, Quaker or Mennonite, evangelical or Baptist—voices speaking out of rich but different traditions.

How is it possible that a church born in an academy, a church whose founders were committed to both the earthly and heavenly kingdom—how could the university academicians of such a church lose their scholarly edge with respect to the engagement of paradox? Was Hughes right—that we dissolved the paradox by pursuing the earthly kingdom to the exclusion of the heavenly thus sliding into what he called a "flaccid, secular ideology"? Indeed, some of our institutions revised their statements of self-understanding in the 1970s to declare that they were "first article" institutions and secular learning was their goal. Had we, willy-nilly, set ourselves up for a peaceful takeover by the epistemologists of the Enlightenment? Had we forgotten that earthly and heavenly kingdoms are two dimensions of a single reality? Had the paradigm done us in?

I puzzled my way over questions like these for a long time—it was the quintessential experience of ambiguity, and in that way a very Lutheran experience. In early years, I was helped along the way by people like my senior colleague, physicist Carl Bailey, and my junior colleague, Tom Christenson. Then in more recent years I was assisted by unseen mentors like Richard Hughes who helped us recognize our treasure; like Joseph Sittler who never gave up on the paradox; like Arthur Holmes who inspired and shaped generations of evangelical academics; like Harold Ditmansen whose clear, compelling voice never waivered; like Mark Schwehn who rang the bell for the rising generation with his 1993 book, *Exiles from Eden*; like George Marsden who served notice to the wider audience of intellectuals that a new group of players was now moving into the academic square.

It was clear by the early 1990s that we Lutherans had some catching up to do: first catching up on our theological and intellectual traditions, then catching up on our scholarly capacities and productivity, and finally catching up on our pedagogy—the pedagogy of connection and paradox embedded in our theology and history. The renewal of the Lutheran intellectual tradition that Mark Schwehn has called for and Mark Noll before him, and now Richard Hughes after him, is a work in progress.

We are making progress, facilitated by the demise of the Enlightenment mindset—"another God that failed" in Marsden's words—and by the encouragement of our ecumenical colleagues. This progress is being legitimized each year by the increasing numbers of recognized scholars among us and by the support and encouragement of our church—most especially the Division for Higher Education and Schools —and by the generosity of allies such as Lutheran Brotherhood, the Lilly Endowment, and the Pew Charitable Trusts. I hasten to note that this activity is not some end in itself designed to please us or our students or other constituents. Rather, this activity is undertaken as an expression of our vocation to serve God's call in the world, to claim our Lutheran particularity in responding to that call and, at the same time, transcend that particularity in response to the Gospel.

So much for my biographical note, or, perhaps more fittingly described, my interpretive editorial. Now let me move to more specific matters. First: What can the Lutheran church do to support the Lutheran intellectual tradition in and through its colleges and universities? It can do so by encouraging and supporting efforts to enlist and equip scholars who can engage the issues of a postmodern, post-Christian time, and do so with confidence that is borne out of love for, and knowledge of, the tradition. This is a major undertaking, for many who are in our academy are either unfamiliar with the Lutheran intellectual tradition or uncomfortable with the pedagogy. Many are new to the tradition. Educated in a postmodern consciousness, many of them are open to new epistemologies. For others, the ties to guild and specialty mean that, by both habit and mindset, the Lutheran tradition is a high wall to scale.

But scale it we can and are and must. The church's encouragement and support are both strategic and generative. The Conference on Vocation and the Lutheran Academy of Scholars both have found enthusiastic audiences on our campuses. This makes all the more important our vision of a sustaining Lutheran academy, a network of scholars from Lutheran and non-Lutheran places who share the pedagogy, gathering in print and person and "virtually" to share, critique, and motivate one another.

There is yet more that the church can do to encourage and sustain us. When necessary, it can protect us, particularly when the fruit of our scholarship sours the taste of the broader church. The church can needle us when we need it—when we become self absorbed, overly pedantic, or inattentive to the traditions and needs of the church. The church can affirm us at local, synodical, and regional levels by recognizing and affirming our good work.

Finally, but not of last importance, the church can ask us for insight when and where we are qualified to offer it. It is my sense that in the face of a widening mission and limited resources, this church needs to work its mission in smarter, more integrated ways. This church needs to transcend the silos of divisions, synods, institutions, and congregations. So I encourage the church in all of its expressions to claim and employ our expertise in addressing a range of issues and opportunities.

And so to question two: What can Lutheran intellectuals do to serve the mission of the church? I proceed here out of the experience of Israel and God's affirmation about the essential place of "teachers of wisdom" in the life of the people and in their relationship to God. I will frame my response around the intellectuals' task in four venues: The first of these is the campus square, that is, literally, our campuses; the second is the academic square, that is, the intellectual community defined in its broadest terms; third, the church square, both Lutheran and ecumenical; and finally the public square, where both soul and policy are shaped.

So first, what can Lutheran teachers of wisdom do to serve the church on its college and university campuses? Practicing the scholarship of discovery and teaching in campus settings is crucial. It is where most of us cut our eye-teeth as scholars once our dissertation was well behind us. The early years often determine our scholarly trajectory. Developing such scholarly gifts, informed by Lutheran presuppositions or "Lutheran leanings," can be crucial in shaping our academic careers as well as the character and quality of campus dialogue and teaching. I believe such scholarship shapes campus ethos, curriculum, and pedagogy. Without thoughtful, informed scholarly reflection the Lutheran light dims and with it a distinctive academic quality. We serve the church best by being lively places of discovery and learning so the campus is the first and primary place in which the Lutheran teacher of wisdom serves the church.

Now to the academic square, where intellectuals gather by disciplines and, increasingly, inter-disciplines, to share intellectual discoveries and advance knowledge. The Lutheran task is to affirm, encourage, and engage the earthly kingdom so we are committed to secular scholarship; it is our business. We are called to this as free and bound men and women of faith who possess scholarly gifts. I believe that in this postmodern time the uniqueness of the Lutheran gift is found in our understanding of dialectic, our sense of contingency, our inclination toward the paradoxical, our understanding of the virtues and limits of human reason, and our approach to issues of vocation. These are significant gifts in a postmodern time, a time that underscores the paradoxical nature of reality, the often decisive influence of context, the contingency of human knowledge, and the role of the community in defining truth. As Lutheran teachers of wisdom we can identify with such uncertainties as these, for we have always known about them. But we are not circumscribed by them, for we know the one who is truth, we know the one who ultimately reconciles that which is seemingly irreconcilable, we know the one who creates community and who provides the grace to transcend human contingencies. This postmodern time is a time to rethink old things and it is an opening for Lutheran teachers of wisdom as fundamental issues of meaning and truth are reconsidered.

Now we move to the church square—to the congregations, synods, commissions, divisions, and the daily work of the church. How can the Lutheran teacher of wisdom serve in the church square? First of all, we can serve by cultivating, elaborating, explicating, and exemplifying the Lutheran intellectual tradition. I overhear claims by some that the study of Reformation history and Lutheran apologetics is not receiving the attention in our colleges, universities, and seminaries that it once did and even now merits. While I cannot judge that claim, the mere report jars my church consciousness. If it is so, then we have work to do. And beyond this task internal to the academy, we need to reach out to the church, to the members of this body. The church Lutheran and the church Catholic need to hear the Lutheran story, need to hear it in images and anecdotes appropriate to this age of seekers. So it is incumbent upon us to take up the task of teaching in the church at large. Not every Lutheran intellectual is equipped to do this, but many are by virtue of their experience and effectiveness in working with students.

A second way we can serve in the church square is by helping to tell the gospel story. I believe that both members and religious seekers want to hear the story the church has to tell. In view of the theological and biblical illiteracy of our day, we need scholars and teachers who can approach this task creatively. People overdosed on the materialistic and short term are crying for a calling that is transcendent. We have the gifts to speak to such quests as these. In many places around the nation we are becoming a teaching/learning church where education spans the ages from cradle to grave, where Bible study is vital, and the engagement of the heavenly and earthly kingdoms is a matter of priority. We have gifts to bring to the church in such places, profound gifts. And yes, lessons to learn as well.

A third area in which Lutheran teachers of wisdom may serve the church is by addressing the mission opportunities of the day. The postmodern generation mostly leaves the church. Someone wrote that they prefer God to religion. Martinson, Barna, and Beaudoin get most of the ink here, but some of our young teacher-scholars with expertise in faith development and learning styles are being heard. We need to find ways to teach the young to live faithfully, morally, hopefully, and creatively in the midst of ambiguity. "What an incredible challenge, and the research," says Martinson, "is still fragmented and begging for new voices and diverse expertise." For another example of mission opportunity, consider multicultural outreach. Opportunity abounds. Think about the possibilities if we, as scholars, could get our arms around the learnings of Lutheran Social Service in refugee resettlement and the international and multicultural experience of our schools, colleges, and universities.

Or turning the page again, think about the contributions we are bringing and can bring to the church as it confronts challenge and crisis. The growing shortage of clergy and professional church workers is a challenge to our imagination sufficient unto itself. Or consider issues of family dysfunction and imagine how we might capture the learning of Lutheran Social Service and campus counselors, for example, through our scholarship and teaching.

Then there are the social ministry issues of health care and end of life. The church has often looked to, and continues to look to, Lutheran scholars as it addresses social policy issues ranging from economics to human sexuality. Within the month formal invitations were extended to the colleges and seminaries regarding the forthcoming churchwide study of human sexuality. Then there are the issues that touch the life and conscience of the church: rural poverty, urban despair, school choice and environmental degradation. Our scholarly gifts are considerable and relevant to each of these issues as is our calling to address them.

That brings me to the public square where public opinion and public policy and the public soul are shaped. The issues abound and include the place of government, the meaning of history, the relationship of church and state, just and unjust war, and the paradoxes of faithful living in an amoral time. We continue to be mentored in this square by teachers of wisdom like Marty, Neuhaus, Rasmussen, Peters, Meilaender, and others. Think of the influence of our colleague Martin Marty—his is a hard-won credibility, make no mistake about that. Such gifts need to be nurtured among us, for in this way we serve the church in its gospel mission.

Let me close where we live, for our "ground zero" is the campus. It is the central place of our service to the church. Scott Russell Saunders, English professor at Indiana University and author of *Hunting for Hope: A Father's Journey*, wrote an essay in the Spring 1999 issue of *The Chronicle of Higher Education*. He defined two years ago what I believe is, post-September 11, an even more significant challenge now than it was then. Saunders spoke in secular terms as he described the sensibilities of his thoughtful students. He wrote:

> In their papers, their remarks in class, and in private conversations, increasing numbers of my students confess to feeling overwhelmed by the scale and complexity of the threats facing humankind. They realize that we all share the same ozone layer, all depend on the same over-fished oceans, dwindling forests, thinning top soil, and fouled rivers. And even if in our current prosperity, America seems to be safe from the financial troubles afflicting so many other nations, thoughtful students

commonly feel a moral responsibility for those who are suffering, even while they themselves are flourishing.

Then Saunders goes on to describe a condition that we can all affirm. He says:

> Without ignoring the grave challenges that beset human beings on this battered and crowded planet, we should work hard at teaching the grounds of hope. It seems to me that education ought to be the antidote for the daily barrage of bad news. Knowledge . . . offers us frameworks for making sense of the fragments, ways of gathering them into wholes. Information arouses our feelings; knowledge helps us imagine how we might act. From kindergarten on, the chief business of education is—or should be—to help students build up larger and larger structures of knowledge, to reveal the heft of things and how the parts of the world connect, to show pathways through the woods of bewilderment. I want my students to keep asking the difficult, perennial questions. But when then asked if there is hope for the future, I want them to be able to answer yes, with confidence in their own powers, with complex knowledge of the world, with eagerness for the healing work they may do.

And so to the bottom line of these reflections, which is that ultimately, the role of the Lutheran teacher of wisdom is to build hope; build it out of the resources of the Lutheran intellectual legacy that we claim and celebrate this night.

CHAPTER ELEVEN

Re-Examination and Renaissance: Lilly-Sponsored Studies at the Turn of the Century

In 2003, the Lilly Endowment invited me to prepare a review of studies that they had sponsored over the previous twenty years. The Lilly Endowment has a deep and substantial tradition of encouragement and support for religious higher education in America. Among other activities, they have generously funded a large number and variety of studies. My task in this essay was to take the measure of all of this and identify some conclusions, or points of consensus, emerging from the body of work. It was a taxing yet stimulating assignment.

Church colleges in America have historically served society by providing an education that is shaped by religious insights, values, and goals. Through most of American history, religious categories and values have shaped our culture in powerful ways. We now live in a post-Christian culture in which Christian values and categories, while still present, no longer define the culture in the same way. So we describe ours as a secular society, and our best chroniclers and critics tell us that religious colleges reflect the secular society more than they do the religious character of their heritage or the confessional precepts of their sponsoring churches.

The challenge for the religious college today is to claim or reclaim its authentic religious heart and voice in ways that serve the deepest needs of a restless society whose moral foundations are fragmented and whose vision is unclear. One wonders whether colleges that have been so powerfully shaped by the culture can effectively reclaim their religious character and, even assuming that they are able to do so, whether or not they can be significant agents of change.

I wish to speak to these profound questions through the prism of personal experience, place, and passion, and out of an understanding of the resources scholars have made available to us through projects funded by the Lilly Endowment. I approach this review of the Lilly studies as a student of religious higher education. I graduated from a religious college and, following graduate training, spent my career as a teacher, dean, and president of a religious college. I am a product of the *logos* of the enlightenment, the *ethos* of a self-consciously religious institution, and the *pathos* of an unreserved loyalty to the place of religious higher education. The reconciliation of these interior dimensions of my vocation in the last decades of the twentieth century was a lively and renewing dialectic. I discovered that numerous colleagues shared this experience. This led me to a sustained period of study and reflection and a deep appreciation for the resources provided by Lilly-sponsored work.

At the start of comprehending the work with which the Lilly Endowment has been associated, it is useful to associate major topics with principal investigators. George Marsden (*Soul*), Douglas Sloan, and Mark Schwehn have provided the leadership in the discussion of the changing intellectual context. Phillip Gleason, Alice Gallin (*Independence*), Tracy Schier and Cynthia Russett, James Burtchaell, William Ringenberg, and the George Marsden–Bradley Longfield collection represent the historical work. Larry Lyon and Michael Beaty have employed social science methodology to document faculty preferences and practices in selected institutions. Conrad Cherry, Betty DeBerg, and Amanda Porterfield used a variety of methodologies in mapping student attitudes and practices on four campuses. Richard Hughes and William Andrian, Robert Benne, and James Burtchaell provided descriptive maps of a number of colleges. The discussion of church relationships is a significant feature of the work of Alice Gallin (*Negotiating*) and Phillip Gleason with respect to Catholic higher education and of Merrimon Cuninggim with respect to the broader group of religious colleges. The work of George Marsden (*Idea*), Douglas Sloan, Mark Schwehn, David O'Brien, Bridget Puzon, and the Stephen Haynes and Andrea Sterk collections reflect new and emerging academic paradigms. The discussion of new practices and strategies includes the work of Benne, Sandra Estenek and Martin Larrey, Arthur Holmes, Richard Hughes, Hughes and Andrian, and Donald Kirby.

While the principal subject matter of this essay is provided by the work sponsored by the Lilly Endowment, other relevant work will also be cited. This essay does not purport to provide a critical review of all of the Lilly-sponsored scholarship because excellent and multiple reviews of most of these studies are already available to the reader. Rather, this essay will identify the themes and insights that I have found most useful in assessing the viability of Christian colleges as a social and cultural force in America. To that end, the essay will explore key markers in the twentieth-century story of religious higher education, the challenge of contemporary academic heterodoxy, and strategies for claiming and sustaining vibrant religious colleges.

Key Markers in the Twentieth Century Story of Religious Higher Eeducation

These markers are useful in gaining some comprehension of the changes experienced in the religious academy in the past century. Taken together, they help explain why religious considerations have marginal influence in the life of the academy in general, and a declining influence in religious colleges in particular.

The hegemony of modernist ways of knowing and claiming truth. With roots in the Renaissance and commitment to reason as its hallmark, modernism gained sway over the academy beginning in the seventeenth century and came to full flower in the twentieth century. The scientific method was established as the preferred epistemology, and pragmatism became the operating paradigm. Institutions were "set free" from confessional limitations, the status of the individual was enhanced, and humanistic and religious ways of knowing were crowded to the periphery. The evolution and impact of modernism on the research universities is masterfully detailed in George Marsden's landmark work, *Soul*. In his view, Protestantism contributed to the disestablishment of the religious voice by identifying its goals too closely with the goals of Western civilization. The epistemology of science led to a "methodological secularization" that excluded religious perspectives from the academic conversation. Many share Marsden's view "that the largely voluntary and commendable disestablishment of religion has led to the virtual establishment of nonbelief, or the near exclusion of religious perspectives from dominant academic life." In this academic environment, excellence was defined by modernist criteria.

Mark Schwehn's work shares in common with Marsden's a consideration of both secular and sectarian institutions. While Marsden shapes his story around the declining influence of Protestant religious values and perspectives and the emergence of secularism, Schwehn focuses on the evolution of the academic vocation, a calling foreshortened by the post-Weberian preoccupation with the creation of knowledge at the expense of discovering truth and moral formation. While Schwehn is concerned about the objectivist epistemology that now dominates the university, his antidote, as we shall see, is more about community and hermeneutics than epistemology.

Douglas Sloan picks up the story of the ascent of modernism in Protestant colleges. The rising neo-orthodoxy in theology encouraged the dialogue between faith and learning early in the last century. Ferment in the church and on church college campuses provided the context for major faculty development activities. The idea was to invigorate the growing education establishment through theologically committed and equipped individuals who could model and lead the integration of faith and learning. But for Sloan, the real challenge was to bridge the intellectual divide between scientific and religious epistemologies, a task at which neo-orthodox theologians such as Paul Tillich and H. Richard and Reinhold Niebuhr tried but failed. The result, according to Sloan, is a two-realm theory of truth in which faith and learning rarely intersect. William Cohoy (Haynes) details some of the consequences. In a two-realm religious college, it is all right for persons to express their religious commitments relative to how they may "feel" about or "value" what they know, but those commitments may not be brought to bear on the "knowing" itself. In religious colleges operating out of the modernist fact/value distinction, "the college's church relationship is seen as relevant to such values and is operative institutionally, often to powerful effect, in the domains of campus ministry, student life, or maybe the theology and religion department. However, it is commonly assumed that the religious commitment and the church-relationship have no place in the classroom, laboratory, or studio where knowledge is sought and taught."

Phillip Gleason tells the Roman Catholic story with a thorough account of how shifting theological and ecclesiastical winds shaped, and were shaped by, the campus and the culture. The Catholic idea early in the century was to reorder society and culture with a Christian vision. In his words: "It came to be regarded as axiomatic by educated Roman Catholics that Thomism provided a rational justification for religious faith, (and) supplied the principles of applying faith to personal and social life." Neo-Scholasticism provided a comprehensive worldview and a unifying academic pedagogy. By the 1950s, for a variety of cultural and ecclesiastical reasons, the Catholic educational establishment became restive about its methodology. There was a desire to break out of it, to connect with the academic mainstream where Catholic intellectuals and institutions were often marginalized. Vatican Council II encouraged these developments. In consequence, the Catholic intellectual/academic project would become more reflective of the modernist paradigm with both its risks and rewards.

The socialization of the faculty around the modernist/objectivist paradigm is the logical outcome of these developments. Many of the Lilly historical accounts tell a familiar story of graduate students being shaped by the academic culture and expectations of research universities in which modernist values and practices prevailed. While not disdaining the values of Enlightenment learning that are foundational to solid academic work, the bias toward scientific ways of knowing is communicated from one generation of academic mentors to the next. The research of Larry Lyon and Michael Beaty bares out the reality of the two-realm theory of truth on the campuses of three widely-recognized religious colleges. Even religiously informed and sympathetic faculty members have difficulty seeing ways in which faith and learning can be integrated in their work. When discovery of knowledge (research) is the penultimate value of one's mentors, it places pressure on one's commitment to the values, piety, and priorities of a religious college. Michael Beaty, Todd Buras, and Larry Lyon (*Faith*) conclude that "as long as the faith and knowledge epistemological crisis remains unsolved, being a modern university will mean separating one's religious commitment from the central tasks of the modern university – the acquisition and transmission of knowledge."

Moving from the academy to the surrounding culture, one recognizes the powerful influence of material, individualistic, instrumental, and pluralistic values. Again, the historical accounts note the influence of a culture hungry for economic development, students motivated by narrow vocational goals (i.e. careers), and a society preoccupied with glitz, consumption, and personal happiness. Many see a connection between these goals and the intellectual values that privilege the pragmatic, the material, and the individual. The cause of concern is not that material and personal issues are to be ignored but rather that they are not contextualized within broader, transcendent values. Consequently, the two realms, faith and action, are unequal and largely disconnected.

Another word about pluralism: The constructive value of pluralism is not the issue, but the relationship between pluralism and particularity is. The idea that we are a richer society because of the plurality of voices and visions is borne out by our history. Bias and discriminatory practices have often jeopardized that richness and have led many to eschew any particularity, be it religious, ethnic, gender, etc. The challenge for a democratic society is to honor the particularities that bring richness to our plurality. The challenge for religious colleges with particular legacies is to sustain and enrich their particularity as they engage the pluralism. This requires courage, integrity, humility, and respect for others.

The other dimension of pluralism, as discussed by Marsden (*Soul*), relates to academic methodologies as represented by both modernism and postmodernism, a matter to which we will turn our attention in a subsequent discussion.

Another pivotal development in the twentieth century story of church colleges is their growth in autonomy. The Alice Gallin volume (*Negotiating*) tells the story of Roman Catholic colleges in terms of laicization, the transfer of ownership and responsibility from the hierarchy to the laity of the church. This development has many roots, including the societal pressures on behalf of academic responsibility and autonomy, the ambitions and visions of educational leaders, and the inclinations of the post-Vatican II church to enfranchise the laity in more powerful ways.

Merrimon Cuninggim's book fills in the broader picture of religious colleges (though without the historical detail of Gallin). He reviews the growth in the autonomy of religious colleges. In the church–college relationship, the colleges were the senior partners by the end of the century. With growing autonomy, in most cases, came increases in quality and public respectability. Clearly, the secularization of the academy and culture shaped the framework for the growing separation of church and college. Beyond Gallin's work and an essay by Beaty (Dovre) tracking recent developments among Southern Baptist colleges, changes in other denominations are not well documented.

As one tracks the weakening of mainline denominational structures in the last third of the century, decreased financial support often translated into diminished leverage in the governance of institutions. As colleges improved their financial capacity, they began to exercise their governance muscle. This meant that as colleges became more assertive about their claims for academic freedom and quality, there was less resistance from the church. Money aside, many church leaders educated in the modernist university were, over time, less convinced of the unique intellectual and religious claims of their colleges. Cuninggim saw a substantial net gain as the colleges became the senior partners in the relationship. Gleason and Gallin take a more balanced view recognizing, on the one hand, the inevitability and institutional advantage of growing independence and, on the other, the desire to maintain a meaningful and integral relationship with the font of substantial intellectual and spiritual resources.

Some institutions in the Protestant sector maintain strong and mutually affirming relationships with their sponsoring churches. One sees examples among Evangelical, Baptist, Lutheran, and Reformed colleges. But, again, the stories within most denominational sectors are not well documented. In addition, there is a lack of studies exploring and documenting new relationship strategies at a time when most denominations are looking for the sort of servant–partners that many colleges are longing to be.

The secularization of religious colleges was the consequence of influences in the broader culture already cited. In addition, certain events and values more specific to campus life had a profound influence on these institutions. As Gleason wrote:

> The coming together of the racial crisis, bitter internal divisions over the Vietnam War, campus upheavals, political radicalism associated with the New Left, the growth of the counterculture, and the emergence of new forms of feminism made the 1960s an epoch of revolutionary change for all Americans.

In addition, nearly all religious colleges sought to establish their nonsectarian character in order to qualify for federal student aid funds. In order to meet institutional funding needs, colleges sought to broaden their constituent base, generalize their mission statements, and impress foundation and corporate funders. In the face of changing demographics and incredible growth, many colleges sought to position themselves in a more ecumenical, less particularist mode.

The effects of modernism and secularism were ameliorated on the campuses of many religious colleges for a considerable period of time through the ethos of the faculty who were part of the tradition, through relationships with sponsoring church bodies, and through religious rituals and traditions. But in much of religious higher education the practice of maintaining a critical mass of denominational communicants on the faculty was diminished on account of the professionalization of the faculty, the shortage of candidates from sponsoring church bodies, the desire for diversity, and the leadership practices of the colleges. In addition, in loco parentis policies, often based on religious values and the expectations of sponsoring churches, were diminished or abandoned all together. To balance the story, it is generally affirmed that most religious colleges made substantial progress in both academic freedom and quality. (This is not to suggest that the goals of religious identity and academic quality are mutually exclusive.)

Lilly scholars offer differing interpretations of these events and their outcomes. Cuninggim brings an essentially positive account of this period, based primarily on the improvements in academic freedom and quality. But most reviews of the period, especially those by Gleason, Sloan, and Burtchaell, render darker judgments. Gleason's observation is representative: "As institutions, most Catholic colleges and universities weathered the storm. But institutional survival in the midst of ideological collapse left them uncertain of their identity. That situation still prevails." It should be noted that David O'Brien offers a more nuanced interpretation of the Catholic experience.

The Lilly studies are perhaps strongest in documenting the trajectories of Catholic colleges as seen in the work of Gleason, Gallin, and the Tracy Schier and Cynthia Russett collection of essays. While Burtchaell's work includes a number of Protestant colleges, no Lilly studies (or other studies of which I am aware) provide the sort of comprehensive analysis of, say, Lutheran, Baptist, Presbyterian, Reformed, Methodist, or evangelical colleges that Gallin, Gleason, and Schier and Russett provide for the Catholic sector.

This essay, as well as the studies cited, masks the reality of the diversity in institutional stories. One explanation does not fit the whole. For example, while Catholic and liberal/mainline Protestant colleges were experiencing separation from historic ties and religious character, the evangelical colleges were experiencing a period of marked growth and vitality beginning in the 1980s and continuing to the present.

The postmodern critique. In the closing decades of the twentieth century, the foundations of modernism were shaken from both inside and outside academe. As citizens sought a deeper sense of meaning and understanding (the "spiritual dimension" as some call it), the modern, objectivist-oriented academy was found wanting. As social/human crises continued unabated in a time of technological mastery, modernism's vulnerabilities became apparent. As the marginalized voices of women, the poor, and persons of color were raised, the objectivist project began to shake. While these external realities were being made manifest, the academy engaged in its own self-critique. The relationship between perspective and perception, between experience and knowing, between motivation and judgment, and between narrative and truth raised serious questions about the modernist project in general and meta-narratives, including Christian, in particular. The combination of new voices, fault lines in the social order, and the self-searching of the academy created a kind of epistemic, hermeneutical chaos. Critics complained of an incipient relativism that would lead to still more chaos. Some predicted the undermining of rationality itself and the descent into nihilism. But others saw the postmodern critique as an invitation to new voices in the academic process and new definitions of the academic project.

The renaissance of religious intentionality in the academy. The last decade of the twentieth century has been a watershed period for students and practitioners of religious higher education in America. Certain crises in the culture, the changing expectations and priorities of religious bodies that sponsor colleges, and the critical re-examination of intellectual paradigms are among the key markers of this watershed. In addition, the systematic and landmark work of the Lilly Endowment has provided the essential resources and marshaled the competent talent that are prerequisite to a sustained and unfolding treatment of these developments.

But behind these developments lie the memory of a rich heritage, the restlessness of academics trying to come to terms with the discontinuities between experience and conviction, and the work of the divine Spirit. The results are many and diverse; we see faculty renewal projects, the emergence of a robust scholarship in faith and learning, the reformulation of institutional missions, the reconsideration of religious identity, curriculum reform, the reshaping of campus life, the re-emergence of religious symbols, and new forms of relationship with the church.

While it is difficult to track beginnings, the emergence of the Coalition of Christian Colleges and Universities in the 1980s was a signal that evangelical colleges intended to be serious about both faith and learning, and they would do it together. Several Protestant church bodies and college clusters initiated studies of mission and identity in the late 1980s. But the momentum grew exponentially in the 1990s when the work of Burtchaell (*First Things*), Marsden-Longfield, Marsden (*Soul*), Schwehn, and Sloan attracted a large and engaged readership. For many readers these authors gave voice and name to realities they had experienced but had been unable to express with such thought and care. Each of these works produced good dialogue and debate over both substance and nuance. Taken together, these works were the flame that illumined new possibilities, and the renaissance was underway.

Navigating Academic Heterodoxy

The confluence of modernist and postmodernist streams of intellectual construction has created an academic whirlpool. Christian apologists seeking a credible role in the academy may choose from among several options and must, therefore, contend with many competing constructions of reality. Marsden (*Idea*) believes that the pluralism of postmodernity opens the door for religious perspectives. He does not ask for any epistemic exception, only a chance to bring a Christian voice to the table, one reflective of a distinctive worldview and values, but susceptible to the usual canons of truth in the academy. Sloan believes epistemology is the key to the intellectual re-engagement of faith and learning. He proposes a new, qualitative epistemology that would be accepting of multiple voices in the service of new ways of knowing and establishing truth. Schwehn seems less interested in epistemology than in hermeneutics. While he does not deny the epistemological hurdle posed by modernism/objectivism, he sees the antidote in a redefinition of the academic calling in the context of a community that values and practices humility, faith, self-sacrifice, and charity.

Writers in the Lilly-sponsored volumes edited by Sterk, Puzon, and Haynes see the postmodern critique as an invitation to new voices and creative strategies. For example, writing in the Haynes collection, Margaret Falls-Corbitt suggests that "postmodern epistemologies, held consistently to their own premises, will prove more favorable to 'reprivileging' the Christian tradition." Marsha Bunge (Haynes) argues that while modernist ways continue to separate faith and learning in the academy, the postmodern situation has made us more aware and appreciative of "the other" and our students more curious about religious questions. Maria Riley, writing in the Puzon volume, speaks of "the embodied intellectual life" as a special insight and contribution that women religious intellectuals bring to the postmodern conversation. In Riley's view, for feminists, the life of the mind cannot be separated from "the emotive, intuitive, physical, experiential, and connected." Women academics bring a different set of experiences to their scholarship. The challenge is to understand how those differences function and to develop an epistemology that demonstrates their truth and significance.

One may claim that postmodernism can help us recognize and reclaim significant elements of our tradition that were marginalized by the hegemony of modernism and the culture of materialism. The significance of community, the power of narrative, the dynamics of place, the significance of values, and the role of pathos are among the beneficiaries of the postmodern consciousness. Schwehn's call for a renewed sense of academic vocation, lived out in a community anchored in core values, is one example of an appropriation of both modern and postmodern insights. Another is William Cohoy's (Haynes) insight about the locatedness of knowing that is, in his view, unavoidable: "What we see is relative to where we stand." Drawing on Alistair MacIntyre's work, Cohoy notes that knowledge rooted in "a place, in narrative, tradition, and community . . . may be authentic and may disclose reality." One may argue with people from other places by entering "empathetically and imaginatively into the language and form of life of the other community, learning that some things are simply untranslatable. On this basis one can begin to understand the other and even make a case for the rational superiority of one tradition over another."

The challenge of heterodoxy is unavoidable for the contemporary scholar, and Richard Bernstein (Sterk) argues for an "engaged fallibilistic pluralism." What makes it fallibilistic is its rejection of "all forms of fundamentalism that appeal to absolute certainty—whether they be religious or secular." It requires "the cultivation of a set of virtues and practices: a willingness to listen to others and to resist the temptation to impose one's own favored categories, standards, and prejudgments; an imaginative hermeneutical sensitivity directed toward understanding what confronts us as radically different; a willingness to defend our beliefs and claims when challenged; the courage to give up our most cherished beliefs when they are seriously called into question. The term 'engaged' is perhaps most important because it implies real encounter, a serious effort to understand what is other and different."

Claiming and Sustaining a Vibrant Religious Character

The historical and critical studies included in the Lilly body of scholarship provide helpful insights about the geneses of our current predicament. Clearly, the burden of the Lilly project in Christian higher education is to envision and embody a vibrant and faithful future for religious colleges. A number of useful models and projects have been identified.

Certain prerequisites of vibrant religious character emerge. Foremost is the need for *vision*. In Benne's view: "The vision is Christianity's account of reality. It is a comprehensive account encompassing all of life; it provides the umbrella of meaning under which all facets of life and learning are gathered and interpreted." One of the most captivating visions for a Christian college is Schwehn's idea of academic vocation, a vision that may be applied to the callings of a college and its faculty, staff, students, and constituents. The goal of the academic vocation is the discovery of truth and moral formation in a value-based community. In another setting, Newman (Haynes) offers a covenantal understanding of vocation that "moves beyond the dichotomy between faith and knowledge." Vocation is a religious concept with theological substance, a vision capable of rallying diverse elements in common cause. Vocation may be expressed in the form of mission statements, vision statements, and learning goals, etc.—all of which make it a rich and useful grounding tool.

Paralleling institutional vision is the necessity of an underlying *worldview*. Richard Mouw, Marsden (*Idea*), and other reformed scholars argue for a Christian worldview that engages and transforms the culture; Schwehn and other Lutherans operate from a two kingdom view and advocate a dialectical engagement between faith (the heavenly kingdom) and the secular order (the earthly kingdom). O'Brien and other Catholics envision a sacramental worldview in which the mutual encounter with Christ is the key to insight and truth. Again, there is rich imagery and insight for the religious academy from these and other worldview formulations.

A third prerequisite for sustaining a vibrant religious college is the experience of a *profound sense of community*. In Cohoy's view (Haynes):

> If all knowing is rooted in some sustaining commu-
> nity, as postmodernists contend, then the
> church-related college becomes not an anomaly or even
> the oxymoron some would claim but a variation on
> the structure common to all knowing and all colleges.

Clearly, a college's vision and worldview shape its understanding and experience of community.

Another prerequisite for vibrant religious colleges is *a shared sense of values*. Schwehn and Cuninggim each provide useful vocabularies of values in their respective works. Paul Lakeland (Haynes) speaks of empathy as a favored (value) method of postmoderninty. He believes that inquirers must "in a real way *love* the object of inquiry; what is to be studied must be respected, allowed, as it were, to be itself." And an important corollary is that such empathy "should be extended (by the scholar) to the religious traditions and identity of the church-related institution itself."

Models of Christian higher education have been set out by a number of Lilly authors. Best known is the work by Hughes and Adrian that describes in a sympathetic way the educational patterns of seven religious traditions. Benne examines six colleges and identifies concrete strategies for building and sustaining Christian character around vision, ethos, and people who bare that vision and ethos. In addition, Mark Roche, Joel Carpenter, Mark Schwehn, Judson Carlberg, Samuel DuBois Cook, and Paul Keim (Dovre) sketch alternative ways to embody religious mission.

Because faculty, more than anyone else, embody and transmit the Christian character of an institution, *faculty development* activity is crucial to the future. According to Haynes: "Faculty involvement is a necessary condition for meaningful religious identity and in certain situations may be a sufficient condition as well." To put it another way, the only people who can bridge the two-realm paradigm are the faculty who are its products and now our teachers. The Lilly Endowment is seriously committed to faculty and staff development. It has sponsored the *Collegium* faculty initiative of the Jesuit Colleges (Thomas Landa), the Rhodes Consultation (Haynes), the Lilly Fellows network, and a staff development program for student affairs professionals (Sandra Estanek and Martin Larrey). Given the interest and the variety of staff development models in place, a comprehensive and published assessment of these projects will be helpful.

Scholarly reflection has come in for special attention in the Lilly work. Marsden (*Idea*), Mouw, and O'Brien have affirmed the essential importance of the Christian academic tradition and the need for the engagement of faith and learning through high-quality scholarship. The Haynes volume brings the voices of younger scholars into this intellectual engagement while the Sterk collection includes recognized scholars representing both secular and sectarian perspectives. In addition, individual institutions, foundations, and denominations are sponsoring ongoing scholarly engagement through, for example, the Pew Younger Scholars Program, the Calvin College Faculty Seminar in Christian Scholarship, the Baylor Institute for Faith and Learning, The Lutheran Academy of Scholars, and many more. These activities reflect the conviction that the intellectual engagement of religion and the broader culture, modern and postmodern, is essential to a vital Christian academy.

A few academic program initiatives are represented in the Lilly collection. For example, O'Brien identifies Catholic Studies initiatives at a number of Catholic colleges; Bunge (Rhodes) lays out a proposal for the religion requirement that includes world religions, Christianity, and ethics; Donald Kirby writes about values-focused programs; and Diane Winston assesses the dynamics of religious identity in adult degree programs at selected church colleges. Missing in the current literature is a report on the large-scale Lilly initiative on vocation (which is understandable because the initiative is still in its early stages). The Lilly initiative is distinctive in that it moves beyond religion requirements or special programs in seeking academic engagement that transcends the two realms segregation typical of the modern academy. No doubt there are scores of institutionally-based curricular initiatives not included in the current literature, and one hopes that future studies will assess and disseminate the results of these activities. We also take note of several religious study programs and centers and endowed professorships that focus on particular religious traditions or academic values.

The literature on new approaches to the *relationship between colleges and sponsoring church bodies* is sparse. In describing the archetype church-related college, Cuninggim gave only brief attention to this matter. The most sustained consideration has occurred in Catholic higher education in response to *Ex Corde Ecclessia* (Gallin). Several Baptist colleges have been involved in the revision of relationships with sponsoring church bodies. Constructive conversation around issues of mission and relationship has taken place in many quarters. But beyond that there has been little concerted exploration and development of new patterns of church and college relationships. This is an important subject both because of a shared mission agenda and because the church provides intellectual and spiritual resources that speak to the integrity of the colleges. In addition, the altered circumstances of both church and college in the twenty-first century suggest that the search for synergies will convey mutual benefits.

To end where I began, the challenge for the religious college is to exercise an authentic heart and voice in ways that serve the deepest needs of a society whose moral foundations are fragmented and whose vision is unclear. Much of the credit for the current renaissance in religious colleges should be extended to the Lilly Endowment. The scope and quality of their sponsored work is outstanding. In tracking the evolution of the body of literature coming out of Lilly research, one notices the maturation of scholarly insight and strategies of change.

In the first section of this essay I identified the markers in the evolution of religious colleges in the last century. Let me close by setting out what I believe will be the markers of vibrant religious colleges in the opening decades of the new century:

1. A reinvigorated sense of vocation for colleges, faculty, students, and constituents. The idea of vocation is a privileged resource in the Christian tradition. Drawing on unique traditions and convictions, it transcends and informs the categories of mission, identity, and vision, and therefore has enormous power in unifying and shaping academic communities.

2. Strong academic communities that share core values and practices. The Christian tradition is rich in resources that are both useful and appropriate to religious colleges. There is particular richness in

the variety of ways in which particular religious traditions emphasize and embody such values and practices.

3. A professorate equipped to navigate the new academic heterodoxy and bridge the two-realm theory of truth in the classroom. The faculty development projects currently underway are absolutely critical if institutions are to fulfill their role in society. This is a particularly difficult challenge given the long period of modernist hegemony that we have experienced.

4. Effective engagement in the scholarly conversation. Scholars from religious colleges need to be "in the game." Reformed and Roman Catholic scholars have set an example. If we believe that we apprehend truth in a particular sphere of inquiry or application, we must speak wherever conversations about truth take place. And we should prepare ourselves to do so with careful attention to the canons of the academy and the disciplines of the scholarly life.

5. Academically sophisticated and mission-savvy leadership. We will need presidents, deans, and board chairs who understand what is at stake, who can and will speak the truth in such matters, and who have the energy and vision to provide effective leadership.

6. Effective engagement with the growing sources of spirituality in the culture. I believe that a new generation of seekers is at the doorstep of the academy. These seekers are more inclined toward the concrete and experiential than toward the abstract and conceptual; they are more open to the religious, the spiritual, and the divine; and they are looking for spiritual/religious integrity in their teachers and mentors, and in their own lives.

7. Effective partnerships with sponsoring religious bodies. It is time to let go of the tensions, some of which are parochial and others not, that mark past relationships. The postmodern and secular circumstances of the new century challenge religious colleges and their sponsoring church bodies to reformulate relationships around unique needs and resources, and shared goals. Rightly configured, new synergies will emerge that enrich both partners.

Works Cited

Michael Beaty, Todd Buras, and Larry Lyon, "Challenges and Prospects for Baptist Higher Education," *The Southern Baptist Educator* 61, no. 4 (April/May/June 1997): 3-6.

Michael Beaty, Todd Buras, and Larry Lyon, "Faith and Knowledge in American Higher Education: A Review Essay," *Fides et Historia* 29, no. 1 (Winter/Spring 1997): 73-80.

James Tunstead Burtchaell. *The Dying of the Light: The Disengagement of Colleges and Universities from Their Christian Churches* (Grand Rapids: Wm. B. Eerdmans Pubishing Co., 1998).

James Tunstead Burtchaell, "The Decline and Fall of the Christian College I," *First Things*, no. 12 (1991): 16-29.

James TunsteadBurtchaell, "The Decline and Fall of the Christian College II," *First Things* no. 13 (1991): 30-38.

Conrad Cherry, Betty A. DeBerg, and Amanda Porterfield, *Religion on Campus* (Chapel Hill: University of North Carolina Press, 2001).

Merrimon Cuninggim, *Uneasy Partners: The College and the Church* (Nashville: Abingdon Press, 1994).

Paul J. Dovre, ed., *The Future of Religious Colleges* (Grand Rapids: Wm. B. Eerdmans Publishing Co., 2002).

Sandra M. Estanek and Martin F. Larrey, "ISACC: Integrating Student Affairs Practice and Catholic Identity," *Current Issues in Catholic Education* 18, no. 2 (Spring 1998): 51-83.

Alice Gallin, *Independence and a New Partnership in Catholic Higher Education* (South Bend, Indiana: University of Notre Dame Press, 1996).

Alice Gallin, *Negotiating Identity: Catholic Higher Education Since 1960* (South Bend, Indiana: University of Notre Dame Press, 2000).

Phillip Gleason, *Contending with Modernity: Catholic Higher Education in the Twentieth Century* (New York: Oxford University Press, 1995).

Stephen Haynes, ed., *Professing in the Postmodern Academy: Faculty and the Future of Church-Related Colleges* (Waco, Texas: Baylor University Press, 2002).

Stephen Haynes, "Teaching Religion at a Church-Related College: Reflections on Professional Identity and Institutional Loyalty" *Religious Studies News* (February 1997): 18-19.

Arthur F. Holmes, *Building the Christian Academy* (Grand Rapids, Michigan: Wm. B. Eerdmans Publishing Co., 2001).

Richard T. Hughes and William B. Adrian, eds., *Models for Christian Higher Education: Strategies for Success in the Twenty-First Century* (Grand Rapids, Michigan: Wm. B. Eerdmans Publishing Co., 1997).

Richard T. Hughes, *How Christian Faith Can Sustain the Life of the Mind* (Grand Rapids, Michigan: Wm. B. Eerdmans Publishing Co., 2001).

Donald J. Kirby, "The Values Program at Le Moyne College," *About Campus* 2, no. 6 (January-February 1998): 15-21.

Thomas M. Landy, "Collegium and the Intellectual's Vocation to Serve," *Conversations on Jesuit Higher Education* 10 (Fall, 1996): pp. 20-29.

Larry Lyon and Michael Beaty, "Integration, Secularization, and the Two-Spheres View at Religious Colleges: Comparing Baylor University with the University of Notre Dame and Georgetown College," *Christian Scholar's Review* 29, no. 1 (Fall 1999): 73-112.

George M. Marsden, *The Soul of the American University: From Protestant Establishment to Established Unbelief* (New York: Oxford University Press, 1994).

George M. Marsden, *The Outrageous Idea of Christian Scholarship* (New York: Oxford University Press, 1997).

George M. Marsden and Bradley J. Longfield, eds., *The Secularization of the Academy* (New York: Oxford University Press, 1992).

Richard J. Mouw, "Christian Scholarship: The Difference a Worldview Makes," *The Cresset*, 60, no. 7 (Special Issue, 1997): 5-14.

David O'Brien, "A Catholic Future for Catholic Higher Education: the State of the Question," *Catholic Education: A Journal of Inquiry and Practice* 1 (September, 1997): 37-50.

Bridget Puzon, ed., *Women Religious and the Intellectual Life: The North American Achievement* (San Francisco: International Scholars Publication, 1996).

William C. Ringenberg, *The Christian College: A History of Protestant Higher Education in America* (Grand Rapids, Michigan: Wm. B. Eerdmans Publishing Co. 1984).

Tracy Schier and Cynthia Russett, eds., *Catholic Women's Colleges in America.* (Baltimore and London: Johns Hopkins University Press, 2002).

Mark Schwehn, *Exiles from Eden: Religion and the Academic Vocation in America* (New York: Oxford University Press, 1993).

Douglas Sloan, *Faith and Knowledge: Mainline Protestantism and American Higher Education* (Louisville, Kentucky: Westminster/John Knox Press, 1994).

Andrea Sterk, ed., *Religion, Scholarship and Higher Education: Perspectives and Directions for the Future* (Notre Dame: University of Notre Dame Press, 2002).

Diane Winston, *The Mission, Formation and Diversity Report: Adult Degree Programs at Faith-Based Colleges* (Princeton, New Jersey: Center for the Study of Religion, Princeton University, 1999).

The Vocation of a Lutheran Liberal Arts College — Revisited

Concordia College Opening Faculty-Staff Workshop
August 22, 2003

In 2003, I was back on campus as Concordia's interim president. Already in place for the coming academic year was a series of reflections on the role of a Lutheran liberal arts college in a changing world. I agreed to address this subject at the opening faculty workshop. It was a fresh opportunity to think about Concordia in terms of the postmodern conversation, the revived understanding of vocation, and the rediscovery of the richness of the Lutheran tradition. One will note echoes from the preceding essay/review of Lilly funded studies. I regard this address as the most comprehensive and cogent expression of my academic credo.

I will take this opportunity to discuss the research I have been involved in recently with a focus on the Lutheran liberal arts tradition.

In the spirit of that tradition, what I share now should be seen more as a series of hypotheses rather than a set of declarations in the sense that Lutheran colleges are very diverse in what and how they appropriate the elements of the tradition. There is not, in any sense, an official Lutheran theological perspective anymore than there is a normative Lutheran liberal arts tradition.

The Lutheran commitment to learning dates from the Reformation itself. Luther exemplified St. Anselm's dictum that "faith seeks understanding." It was intellectual inquiry fed by religious anxiety that led Luther to his breakthrough reading of Romans on the nature of

140 • The Cross and the Academy

salvation. It was Luther's commitment to the laity, the priesthood of all believers, that led him to champion a universal education that would give people of both sexes and all ages direct access to knowledge. It was Luther's commitment to worldly truth that led him to exclaim: "How can you not know what can be known?" It was his respect for human curiosity that led him to write the catechism with its recurrent question: "What does this mean?" following each creedal affirmation. It was commitment to the place of learning in church and world that led Luther and Melanchthon to spearhead a reformation of the curriculum at Wittenberg University. This is a significant history, but what leads us to revisit the vocation of a Lutheran liberal arts college in the first decade of a new century? Let me venture some answers to that question.

The first reason is because, beginning a decade ago, we realized that the vocation of Lutheran liberal arts colleges (and other religious colleges) might be slipping away. As George Marsden related in his epic, *The Soul of the American University*, the hegemony of modernism marginalized humanistic and religious ways of knowing all across the academic landscape. It left religious colleges, at best, with what Douglas Sloan calls a two-realm theory of truth in which faith (values) and learning (facts) rarely intersected. In Mark Schwehns's analysis, the post-Weberian preoccupation with the creation of knowledge edged out the discovery of truth and moral formation as desirable ends of learning. Academic excellence came to be defined by modernist, scientific criteria. Most of us were socialized in the modernist academy, and its methods and values shaped our intelligence. Survey work led by Michael Beaty at Baylor University documents the impact of the two-realm theory of truth upon faculties at three highly-recognized religious colleges and universities.

The recent history of religious colleges has been chronicled by several writers, mostly notably by James Burtchaell in his landmark work, *The Dying of the Light*. As Burtchaell and others note, the straying of colleges from their religious moorings was in some cases a deliberate action of the colleges. For example, in order to meet institutional funding needs, many colleges sought to broaden their constituent base by generalizing their mission statements. In the face of change and incredible growth, many colleges sought to position themselves in a more ecumenical, secular, and less particularist mode. The influence of modernism and secularism was ameliorated on the campuses of many religious colleges for a considerable period of time through the *ethos* of the faculty who were part of the tradition, through relationships with sponsoring church bodies, and through religious rituals and traditions. But over time the rituals and traditions became less evident and important. Along with that, the *ethos* of the faculty was reshaped by professionalization, the shortage of candidates from related church bodies, the desire for diversity, and the leadership practices of the colleges.

A second reason we revisit the vocation of a Lutheran liberal arts college is because of the powerful influence of material, individualistic, instrumental, and pluralistic values in our culture. Again, the historical accounts note the influence of a culture hungry for economic development, students motivated by narrow vocational goals, and a society preoccupied with glitz, consumption, and personal happiness. Many see a connection between these goals and the intellectual values that privilege the pragmatic, the material, and the individual. The cause of concern is not that material and personal issues are to be ignored, but rather that they are not contextualized within broader, transcendent values. Consequently, the two realms, faith and action, are unequal and largely disconnected.

A word about pluralism: The constructive value of pluralism is not the issue, but the relationship between pluralism and particularity is. The idea that we are a richer society today because of the plurality of voices and visions is borne out by our history. Bias and discriminatory practices have often jeopardized that richness and have led many to eschew any particularity, be it religious, ethic, or gender. The challenge for a democratic society is to honor the particularities, the *pluribus*, that bring richness to our *unum*, and the challenge for religious colleges is to sustain and enrich their particularity as they engage the pluralism. This requires courage, integrity, humility, and respect for others.

A third reason we revisit these issues relates to the critique of postmodernism. In the closing decades of the twentieth century, the foundations of modernism were shaken from both inside and outside the academy. As citizens sought a deeper sense of meaning and understanding (the spiritual dimension, as some call it), the modern, objectivist-oriented academy was found wanting. As social/human crises continued unabated in a time of technological mastery, modernism's vulnerability became apparent. As the marginalized voices of women, the poor, and persons of color were raised, the objectivist project began to shake.

While these external realities were being made manifest, the academy engaged in its own self-critique. The relationship between perspective and perception, between experience and knowing, between motivation and judgment, and between narrative and truth raised serious questions about the modernist project in general and other narratives, including Christian, in particular. A combination of new voices, fault lines in the social order, and the self-searching of the academy created a kind of epistemic/hermeneutical chaos. Critics complained of an insipient relativism that would lead to still more chaos. Some predicted the undermining of rationality itself and the descent into nihilism. But others saw the postmodern critique as an invitation to new voices in the academic process and new definitions of the academic project. We have an increasing body of literature from both young and seasoned scholars who are attempting to unpack the epistemological confusion and engage the desperate voices in common dialogue. This is a hopeful sign. (Particularly valuable are *Professing in the Postmodern Academy: Faculty and the Future of Church Related Colleges*, a collection of essays by younger scholars edited by Stephen Haynes, and *Religious Scholarship and Higher Education: Perspectives and Direction for the Future*, the work of established scholars edited by Andrea Sterk.)

The fourth reason we reconsider the vocation of a Lutheran liberal arts college is because of the renaissance of religious intentionality in the culture and in the academy. Speaking of what he calls our smorgasbord culture, Miloslav Volf of the Yale Divinity School observes:

> Communities of faith have not found effective ways
> to offer a compelling vision of an integral way of life
> that is worth living. Many people are seeking precisely
> that. They are unsatisfied with a lifestyle shaped only
> by the watchwords of contemporary culture: "freedom"

and "prosperity." This is signaled by the resurgent interest in spirituality as related to almost every dimension of life—from medicine to business, from arts to politics.

The last decade of the twentieth century has been a watershed for many religious colleges due to the crises in the culture, the changing priorities of religious bodies, and the re-examination of intellectual paradigms noted above. And behind these developments may be found a rich heritage, the restlessness of academics trying to come to terms with the discontinuities between experience and conviction, the growing spiritual self-consciousness of students and younger faculty, and the work of the divine Spirit. The results are many and diverse: We see faculty renewal projects, the re-emergence of a robust scholarship in faith and learning, the reformulation of institutional missions, the reconsideration of religious identity, curriculum reform, the reshaping of campus life, the reemergence of religious symbols and practices, and new forms of relationship with the church.

What then is the vocation of a Lutheran liberal arts college? I believe that it finds its expression in three areas: purpose, substance, and pedagogy. Let me explore each in turn.

1. Purpose. The vocation of a Lutheran college is expressed, first of all, in its purpose, and here the Lutheran idea of vocation is formative. In Luther's view, God takes the initiative in the relationship between God and humans. We receive the righteousness of God through faith. We do not earn it or build our life toward that end. So salvation is our starting point, not the goal of our lives. We receive this gift through faith, and we respond to God's call through our vocation in service to the neighbor. The Lutheran concept of vocation was and is unique, and it begins with gift. In addition, it is distinctive in that it is inclusive of all occupations. Another feature of Luther's formulation is its comprehensiveness. For Luther, vocation was occupation, but it was so much more than that. It was home and family and community and leisure and church—wherever one meets the neighbor. As Mark Edwards put it, "Luther spiritualized secular life, by taking the notion of spiritual calling and applying it to all honest walks of life."

Luther was concerned about the renewal of the church, but his larger concern was the renewal of society. Thus, he was concerned about the education and conduct of those called to be priests and monks, but he was just as concerned for those called to be shoemaker, farmer, judge, parent, and teacher, and so he called all of them priests! The calling to serve the neighbor leads us to issues of love and justice, it leads us to the community, and it leads us to concern for the common good. Again and again, Luther's centering ethic was expressed in the question: "Does it serve the neighbor?"

In view of this, what then is the purpose of a Lutheran liberal arts college? To call and prepare graduates to serve the neighbor. Luther made the case in his letter to the councilmen in 1524 as he wrote:

> In order to maintain its temporal estate outwardly, the world must have good and capable men and women, men able to rule well over land and people, women able to manage the household and train children and servants alike. Now such men must come from our boys, and such women from our girls. Therefore, it is a matter of properly educating and training our boys and girls to that end.

Luther particularly underscored the necessity of good education for those who would be leaders, rulers, and authorities. So again, the vocation of a Lutheran liberal arts college is to call and prepare students to serve their neighbor.

2. Substance. This leads to the second expression of our vocation as a Lutheran liberal arts college, and that is in the substance of the enterprise. Let me say a few things initially about the reformers' commitment to what we refer to as the liberal arts. Martin Luther and Phillip Melanchthon were dismayed by the scholastic curriculum of their day, a curriculum that featured philosophy, a rote dialectic practice, and dogmatic formulations of belief and practice. In the 1524 letter to which I previously referred, Luther lamented about his own education in these words:

> How I regret now that I did not read more poets and historians and that no one taught me them! Instead I was obliged to read at great cost, toil, and detriment

to myself the devil's dung, the philosophers and soph-
ists, from which I have all I can do to purge myself.

In response to this, Luther and Melanchthon said, metaphori-
cally: "Let in the 'light'." It should be noted that the reformers
recognized the power and value of non-Christian contributions to
culture. The great pagan poets and writers were to be taught in schools
partly for their inherent value, partly as instrumental to the mastery
of language and grammar for the study of scripture" (Richard Baepler,
The Lutheran Reader). While Luther disliked Aristotle in general, he
recognized the superior value of his moral ethics. For Luther and the
other reformers at Wittenberg the mantra was "consider history, the
languages and classics, develop critical perspective, study moral philosophy, and learn and practice a rhetoric that engages life." In the
words of James Kittelson, for Luther and other humanists,

> true knowledge was not universal and propositional
> in character, but concrete and specific to time and
> place. Its truths were not *scientia* or knowledge but
> *sapientia* or wisdom, which was to be found in the mar-
> ketplace and in the conduct of daily life rather in the
> lecture hall or the monastery. Education thus had an
> end both temporally and finally. This end was the fin-
> ished person that came out of the classroom and into
> society, the one who could apply general principles in
> a variety of specific situations (James M. Kittleson,
> *Luther and Learning*).

All of this is by way of saying that we have a legacy– a liberal arts
legacy, a legacy of curriculum reform, a legacy that includes both the
sacred and the secular.

But in addition to this liberal arts legacy, the substance of our
collegiate enterprise is shaped by several theological themes and elements. In his book, *Quality with Soul*, Robert Benne writes that one
of the distinctive resources of a healthy religious college is the Christian account of reality. This account is comprehensive, "it provides an
umbrella of meaning under which all facets of life and learning are
gathered and interpreted." It does not claim to have all of the data,
but it offers a paradigm in which data and knowledge about the world

can be "organized, interpreted, and critiqued." This Christian account arises from the Christian narrative and from the intellectual tradition that has emerged from it, and this intellectual tradition, says Benne, "conveys a Christian view of the origin and destiny of the world, of nature and history, of human nature and its predicament, and of the human situation and of the Christian way of life." In other words, the Christian account provides a variety of substantive propositions that may shape the academic experience of a Lutheran college. While it would be presumptuous to even attempt to unpack all of this for our time and place, some illustrations may be helpful—six in all.

We begin with the Christian notion of *freedom* and its profound implications. Saved by grace from the burden of sin and the necessity of constructing our own salvation, we are free to serve God, free to explore all that God has done. This is a more profound notion of freedom than we find any place else in our culture. This leads most naturally to academic freedom, described in the recent draft of the college's statement of purpose as "the exercise of critical inquiry and the use of reason to discover the beauty, complexity, and order in creation and contribute to the emergence of a just world." The practice of free inquiry, a right secured by the secular authorities in Saxony, enabled Luther to unlock the scriptures and emboldened him to set out his arguments for critical examination in the forum of public opinion. It is a legacy with both substantive and pedagogical significance. Indeed, our call to serve the neighbor requires that the truth be discovered and that the truth be told in a society that is always in need of reformation.

A second theme with implications for the substance of our work is Luther's *affirmation of the world*. Luther spoke of a God active in two kingdoms or two realms—the heavenly realm where grace rules and the earthly realm where reason and the law are indispensable. These two kingdoms are both arenas of God's activity, and Christians are called to be active in both. What was distinctive about Luther's view was his affirmation of the world, the secular—his view that this is God's creation and the site of God's continuing activity—and so (as I noted earlier) Luther affirmed the study of so-called pagan authors and understood that they possessed knowledge that was essential in serving the neighbor.

A third substantive theme has to do with the *importance of the arts*. Music, in particular, played a key role in the Lutheran Reformation, more so than in the Calvinist Reformation with its rejection of graven images. So there was a creative explosion in the hymnody as well as a general cultivation of music. "Music not only banished earthly cares and became a vehicle for glorifying God, it seemed to mediate the presence of God in special ways" (Baepler, *The Lutheran Reader*).

A fourth theme is the *centrality of community* in Luther's writing and speaking. The vocation of serving the neighbor brings us into community. Recognizing God's work in the earthly kingdom brings us to community. Confessing the third article of the historic confession of the church leads us to community. Therefore it is not surprising that Lutherans have been distinctive among denominations in their engagement in the public sector. For example, in the United States, Lutherans account for only three percent of the population, but sponsor twenty-five percent of the nursing homes and the largest social and human service enterprise in the nation. In addition, Lutherans have pioneered the development of global assistance through Lutheran World Relief and the Lutheran Immigration Service has resettled more refugees that any agency except the U.S. government.

Moral deliberation of the sort Luther encouraged and exemplified begins with attending to the biblical narrative and the insights of the tradition, and often ends by engaging the reflection and common sense of the community. In Luther's view no particular form of government or public policy was mandated by the Bible or tradition, so we need to use our reason to apply ourselves with wisdom. Luther modeled this paradigm, sometimes well and sometimes badly. Although he did not deny his fallibility, neither did he use it as an excuse for inaction.

A fifth theme is what I describe as a *sense of contingency*. It is expressed in a number of ways, including the famous *simul justis et pecator* formulation, the confession that we are simultaneously both sinner and righteous. We also see it in Luther's view on the limits of reason. Luther viewed reason as "the most important and the highest in rank among all things, and, in comparison with other things of this life, the best and something divine." But he was leery of Erasmus and others who thought they could rationalize divine grace and revelation, and he was sensitive to the ways in which persons who were simultaneously saint and sinner could corrupt reason.

The sense of contingency is also evident in Luther's preference for the paradoxical, the reality of the sometimes irresolvable tension among alternative ways of understanding and negotiating reality. This sense of contingency leads to a sense of intellectual humility. It may also enable Lutheran intellectuals to be less bothered by the epistemic and hermeneutical chaos of postmodernism—but that is the subject for another day. Finally, it perhaps accounts for the "ethical realism" characteristic of Lutherans, the idea that we are called to work for change without the expectation of heaven on earth. This apparently sensible insight has led others to suggest that our "realism" may lead to quietism.

The theology of the cross perhaps best exemplifies the Lutheran sense of contingency. In view of the human suffering we have experienced in the past century and already in this new one, this theme is worthy of our attention. We are called to think *coram deo*, that is, in relationship to God. And we find God in suffering places, places where we encounter most dramatically the limits of human wisdom and action. In weakness we find God's strength; in human folly we find God's wisdom; in the cross we find God's victory. To seek God in such crosses is a profound quest, one that opens us to both spiritual depths and heights, to our own human limitations, and our human possibilities as messengers of God.

A decade ago Nicholas Woltersdorf, a guest on this campus on more than one occasion, lost his son in a mountaineering accident. He experienced a long night of grief. As he emerged from this experience of the cross he wrote:

> To believe in Christ's rising and death's dying is also to live with the power and the challenge to rise up now from all our dark graves of suffering love. If sympathy for the world's wounds is not enlarged by our anguish, if love for those around us is not expanded, if gratitude for what is good does not flame up, if insight is not deepened, if aching for a new day is not intensified, if hope is weakened and faith diminished, if from

the experience of death comes nothing good, then death has won. Then death, be proud.

A sixth substantive resource emerging from the Lutheran tradition is *the incarnation*. Luther's idea was that the finite, that is human beings and other created things, are capable of witnessing to the infinite, which is the divine. As the bread and the wine convey God's gift and presence, as prayer and word give us access to God's spirit, so also does human work in the community make a difference. That work may be making good shoes or good beer, or it may be aiding the poor and disenfranchised, or it may be engaging in the hard and often ambiguous work of moral deliberation, but we are God's creatures who in spite of the dirt on our shoes and in our souls are called and enabled to convey God's truth and mercy in whatever station we may find ourselves.

3. Pedagogy. We have not exhausted the Lutheran themes that may bring substance to a Lutheran liberal arts college, but hopefully, we have exemplified the possibilities. Let me now turn to the third of the ways in which the vocation of a Lutheran liberal arts college may manifest itself, and that is in our pedagogy.

First, from a pedagogical point of view, we are reminded of Luther's high praise for and confidence in *human reason* as a means of understanding God's revelation, and of gaining wisdom and skill to live out our vocation in the world. His reservations about the limits of human reason notwithstanding, Luther and his colleagues had high expectations for the intellectual rigor of their work and the work of their students.

The Lutheran preference for *dialectic* constitutes a second contribution to pedagogy. It is framed by the themes of contingency, the limits of reason, and by our human nature. But it is also shaped by our callings in the world, the need to bring the insights of our faith to bear on the burden of our callings. Returning again to Robert Benne, he argues for a dialectic that will reveal the alternative worldviews that shape our academic disciplines. For example, let the worldview assumptions of classical economics be in conversation with those of Christian ethics, let the disciplinary assumptions of literary criticism be in conversation with those of natural science. If we are to transcend the two-realm theory that dominates the academy, then conversation between the disciplines and the Christian intellectual account, or between faith and learning, is both a promising and necessary activity. From a Lutheran point of view, the objective is not to Christianize or somehow "convert" the disciplines, because we regard them as having integrity in their own right. Rather, the goal is to engage the disciplines in the service of holistic understanding, a holism that recognizes the sacred and secular as two realms of a single reality, that is, God's creation.

A third pedagogical resource is our notion of *paradox*. As noted before, this has strong roots in the substance of the Lutheran theological tradition. But it has pedagogical implications as well. It may provide a modality for understanding complexity and ambiguity. Richard Hughes raises a warning flag worthy of consideration. He points out that while paradox is a unique gift, it is also a weakness. In nurturing both sides of a paradox, it is easy to sacrifice one side for the other. In Hughes words, "when paradox dissolves in this way, the risks can be absolutism on the one hand and relativism on the other." This tendency is especially apparent in considering the Lutheran formulation of two realms. If we accentuate the realm of God, we may absolutize our religious vision as the Scholastics did. On the other hand, if we accentuate the realm of the world, we run the risk of relativism. So our challenge is to maintain the tension. I believe he advises us wisely in this matter.

So in conclusion, for many good reasons Lutheran liberal arts colleges are revisiting their sense and understanding of vocation. The implications go well beyond those noted today, but perhaps this will suffice as a beginning. As academics in a Lutheran setting, we have a goodly treasure.

Let me close with the testimony of one who speaks about our tradition from outside of it, Richard T. Hughes. Here is what he says about us:

> The Lutheran tradition possesses some of the most potent theological sources for sustaining the life of the mind that one could imagine. It encourages a dialogue between the Christian faith and the world of ideas,

fosters intellectual humility, engenders a healthy suspicion of absolutes, and helps create a conversation in which all of the conversation partners are taken seriously.

It seems to me Hughes says it right, and he sets a standard worthy of our highest aspirations.

Works Cited

Michael Beaty, Todd Buras, and Larry Lyon, "Faith and Knowledge in American Higher Education: A Review Essay," *Fides et Historia* 29, no. 1 (Winter/Spring 1997): 73-80.

Robert Benne, *Quality with Soul* (Grand Rapids, Michigan: Wm. B. Eerdmans Publishing Co., 2001).

James Tunstead Burtchaell, *The Dying of the Light: The Disengagement of Colleges and Universities from Their Christian Churches* (Grand Rapids, Michigan: Wm. B. Eerdmans Publishing Co., 1998).

Paul J. Contino and David Morgan, *The Lutheran Reader* (Valparaiso: Valparaiso University, 1999).

Merrimon Cuninggim, *Uneasy Partners: The College and the Church* (Nashville: Abingdon Press, 1994).

Paul J. Dovre, ed. *The Future of Religious Colleges* (Grand Rapids, Michigan: Wm. B. Eerdmans Publishing Co., 2002).

Mark U. Edwards Jr., "Lutheran Leanings," *Dialogue: A Journal of Theology* 41:1 (Spring, 2002): 50-62.

Alice Gallin, *Independence and a New Partnership in Catholic Higher Education* (South Bend, Indiana: University of Notre Dame Press, 1996).

Alice Gallin, *Negotiating Identity: Catholic Higher Education Since 1960* (South Bend, Indiana: University of Notre Dame Press, 2000).

Phillip Gleason, *Contending with Modernity: Catholic Higher Education in the Twentieth Century* (New York: Oxford University Press, 1995).

Marilyn J. Harran, ed., *Luther and Learning* (Selingsgrove, Pennsylvania: Susquehanna University Press, 1985).

Stephen Haynes, ed., *Professing in the Postmodern Academy: Faculty and the Future of Church-Related Colleges* (Waco, Texas: Baylor University Press, 2002).

Arthur F. Holmes, *Building the Christian Academy*. Grand Rapids. Michigan: Wm. B. Eerdmans Publishing Co., 2001).

Richard T. Hughes and William B. Adrian, eds., *Models for Christian Higher Education: Strategies for Success in the Twenty-First Century* (Grand Rapids, Michigan: Wm. B. Eerdmans Publishing Co., 1997).

Richard T. Hughes, *How Christian Faith Can Sustain the Life of the Mind* (Grand Rapids, Michigan: Wm. B. Eerdmans Publishing Co., 2001).

Darrell Jodock, "The ELCA Colleges and the Church: Strengthening the Partnership," Unpublished manuscript, 2002.

Darrell Jodock, "The Lutheran Tradition and the Liberal Arts College: How are they Related?" in *Called to Serve*, Pamela Scwandt, ed. (Northfield, Minnesota: St. Olaf College, 1999).

Darrell Jodock, "Vocational Discernment: A Comprehensive College Program," Unpublished manuscript presented at the ELCA Conference on the Vocation of a Lutheran College, Valparaiso University, 2001.

Luther's Works, Vol. 45.

Larry Lyon and Michael Beaty, "Integration, Secularization, and the Two-Spheres View at Religious Colleges: Comparing Baylor University with the University of Notre Dame and Georgetown College," *Christian Scholar's Review* 29, no. 1 (Fall 1999): 73-112.

George M. Marsden, *The Soul of the American University: From Protestant Establishment to Established Unbelief* (New York: Oxford University Press, 1994).

George M. Marsden, *The Outrageous Idea of Christian Scholarship* (New York: Oxford University Press, 1997).

George M. Marsden and Bradley J. Longfield, eds., *The Secularization of the Academy* (New York: Oxford University Press, 1992).

Richard J. Mouw, "Christian Scholarship: The Difference a Worldview Makes," *The Cresset*, 60, no. 7 (Special Issue, 1997): 5-14.

David O'Brien, "A Catholic Future for Catholic Higher Education: the State of the Question," *Catholic Education: A Journal of Inquiry and Practice* 1 (September, 1997): 37-50.

William C. Ringenberg, *The Christian College: A History of Protestant*

Higher Education in America (Grand Rapids, Michigan: Wm. B. Eerdmans Publishing Co., 1984).

Mark Schwehn, *Exiles from Eden: Religion and the Academic Vocation in America* (New York: Oxford University Press, 1993).

Ernest L. Simmons, *Lutheran Higher Education: An Introduction for Faculty* (Minneapolis: Augsburg Fortress, 1998).

Douglas Sloan, *Faith and Knowledge: Mainline Protestantism and American Higher Education* (Louisville, Kentucky: Westminster/John Knox Press, 1994).

Andrea Sterk, ed., *Religion, Scholarship and Higher Education: Perspectives and Directions for the Future* (South Bend, Indiana: University of Notre Dame Press, 2002).

Miroslav Volf, "Way of Life," *Christian Century* (November 20–December 3, 2002): 35.

Nicholas Wolterstorff, *Lament for a Son* (Grand Rapids, Michigan: Wm. B. Eerdmans Publishing Co., 1987).

CHAPTER THIRTEEN

The Lutheran Calling in Education

The ELCA Conference on Vocation
Capital University, Columbus, Ohio
July 28-31, 2006

In 2004, the Evangelical Lutheran Church in America created a task force to prepare a social statement on education. Such statements provide a guide to church advocacy, church practice, and the stewardship of members. The purview of the statement was comprehensive of public and private education from preschool through graduate and professional education. As co-chair of the task force I was invited to address the ELCA Conference on the Vocation of a Lutheran College, an annual gathering of faculty and staff from ELCA colleges and universities across the country. In this address I rehearsed the charge of the task force, provided a perspective on contemporary challenges facing education, and offered a perspective on our calling in education.

Since its founding, and following the practices of its predecessor church bodies, the ELCA has prepared and adopted social statements on a variety of critical issues from the environment to the economy. Following in this tradition, the ELCA commissioned the preparation of a social statement on education in 2001. The purpose of the statement will be to inform public policy advocacy and provide counsel to the church, its institutions, congregations, and members.

With the goal of producing, reviewing, and adopting a social statement at the Churchwide Assembly in 2006, the Task Force charged with preparation of the statement produced a study document in 2004 and a draft social statement in 2006. In this essay I will undertake three tasks: first, to focus on the current social context and its consequences as a way of identifying some of the issues that the social statement seeks to address; then I will spend a bit of time reflecting on why it is that Lutherans care about such matters; and finally, I will consider some of the prospects and possibilities available to us in addressing the critical issues. Given the nature of my assignment, this will be more of an annotated listing of issues, elements, and resources rather than a substantive philosophical argument.

First then, to *our social context* and some of its consequences. I begin with consideration of young people. In a review of *Soul Searching: the Religious and Spiritual lives of American Teenagers*, Sandra Scofield notes that while eighty-four percent of teenagers say that they believe in God and fifty percent say that faith is extremely important to them, a minority of them regularly practice their faith and have no idea what their parent's religious values are. While the seriously committed "tend to show compassion for others in volunteer activities, do well in school, maintain good family relationships, and avoid drugs and sex," they do not seem able "to tie their sense of moral directives to the teachings of a historical church or orthodoxy that underlies their faith." The result, says Scofield, is that "religion gets interpreted with a template that comes straight from the general culture, with its emphasis on individualism."

The April 15, 2005, issue of the *Chronicle of Higher Education* published a report on the Higher Education Research Institute's study on spirituality in higher education. Among other things, the study authors conclude that "most college freshmen believe in God, but fewer than half follow religious teachings in their daily lives. A majority of first-year students (sixty-nine percent) say their beliefs provide guidance, but many (forty-eight per cent) describe themselves as 'doubting,' 'seeking,' or 'conflicted.'" A related study by UCLA found that the percentage of students who frequently attend religious services shrank from fifty-two percent of incoming freshman to twenty-nine percent of juniors. According to Roland Martinson's research, there is among the young great interest in spirituality, but little interest in knowledge of the faith and the tradition. Too many of the young find the tradition trivial and unengaging, and so their spirituality and morality are shaped by the popular culture.

Meanwhile in the mainline denominations, education and worship get short shrift in comparison to other religious traditions. In a national study of 549 randomly selected and diverse congregations,

Nancy T. Amerman found that "the religious groups that spend the least organizational energy on the core tasks of worship and religious education are the mainline Protestant ones." Small wonder that the mainline church struggles for loyalty, for an evangelical strategy, for an effective educational pedagogy, for a youth strategy, and for leaders and teachers of competence and vision for the work of Christ's mission in church and society.

Unfortunately, the family map features too much brokenness and multi-tasking, too many absent parents and proxy parents, and too little attention to faith and character formation. In Christian families, the vows that parents make regarding the spiritual formation of their children are often neglected or delegated to congregations whose education programs are short on time and leadership.

The next dimension of our context is our *schools*. People are not happy that our schools do not measure up to the performance of schools in other nations. They are unhappy that too many students fail, that there is too much violence in schools, that character formation is being slighted, that school lunch programs do not feature nutritious foods, that there is too much or too little or the wrong kind of attention to sex education, and that special education is receiving either too much or too little of school resources. The public cries for accountability and improvement, and the government responds with No Child Left Behind and a bushel of money that some say is not enough and others say is misdirected. In increasing numbers, special interest groups pursue agendas in behalf of prayer or intelligent design or the teaching of religion.

Teachers are increasingly restive under multiple roles and mandates, particularly about teaching to tests. Educational leaders wonder how to maintain morale and how to attract teachers of good quality in adequate numbers.

While schools continue to be re-segregated in the cities, schools in rural areas fight to sustain viability. The unequal distribution of wealth results in an unequal distribution of financial resources for schools, so equal access to quality education is not the reality, political rhetoric to the contrary notwithstanding. Surely it is not all about money—but yet it is about money.

A third element of this review of context is our *communities*. Robert Bellah and his colleagues did the fundamental diagnostic work two decades ago, and Robert Putnam verified their underlying theses a decade ago. These theses are familiar: Individualism trumps community, feeling good trumps being good, and self-satisfaction trumps altruism. Civility is a rarer commodity than we would wish. Politicians on the left and right are so focused on their respective power bases that their capacity to identify and pursue the common good is increasingly problematic. So the rhetoric is hotter, the tactics less responsible, and all of it is justified according to a Machiavellian calculus.

- We seem increasingly to believe that dollars spent in behalf of the common good would be better spent for the individual good. Of course, misdirected public expenditures are a reality, and governmental reform is a continuing necessity. But the animus to public spending runs deeper than that, so we cut taxes, resist new ones, and refer those that we do pass to public referendum wherever possible.

- The economy is viewed globally and experienced individually. The mantra is that outsourcing is going to create new opportunities for those who are displaced and cheaper, better products for all. While our employment rates remain high, polls tell us that the poor and the middle class are anxious and uncertain about their place in the new global economic order.

- Since September 11 we have experienced a war without lines or borders and a world in which uncertainty and anxiety often transform hospitality into hostility in the case of those who are viewed as different because of color, creed, or culture.

- The realities of diversity in our communities are met with celebration and welcome on the one hand, and with fear and exclusion on the other. The reality of pluralism and multiculturalism is met with relativism or critical tolerance or an anxious and sometimes angry fundamentalism. As if this is not enough to disrupt the human community, advances in science create crises for both patients and practitioners.

The final destination in this environmental scan is *higher education*. Our society is clear that education, and higher education in particular, is the key to the economic well-being of our citizens and our nation state. To that end, we have commodified higher education in the sense that the ultimate measure of its effectiveness is its capacity to fuel the economic engine. To the despair of Lutherans, vocation is equated with career, and education for citizenship is thus marginalized.

Since there is a strong argument that higher education possesses the keys to the economic well-being of our nation and the economic equity of its citizens, then access to education is a high priority. But as costs have escalated, public support and family capacity have not kept pace. Demographers are warning us that if we do not address the educational quality issues in K-12 and the access issues in higher education, then our new Americans and our poorer Americans will not be able to matriculate, and the workforce needs of a high tech society will not be met.

In the wake of modernism, postmodernism, and deconstruction, higher education is a place where soul questions are often either ruled out of order or treated as matters primarily of subjective interest. Our post-Weberian narrowing of the vocation of a scholar as detailed in Mark Schwehn's *Exiles in Eden* is part of this matter, as is the fact/value split (Sloan) and some misconstrual of the doctrine of the separation of church and state. This narrowing of academic vision had a significant and continuing impact in both public and religious higher education (Benne and Marsden). Adding to the stress in the case of religious colleges, including Lutheran, is the declining capacity of the sponsoring church bodies and the consequent rearranging of denominational priorities at the expense of higher education. And so scholars, both young and old, quest for vocations that will, in the words of Gail Godwin, "keep making more of you" (*Evensong*). For all of these reasons, life in the academy in a postmodern, post-Christian, and pluralistic society may be an experience of exile.

But why is this Lutheran church—to which we are connected either as members of the communion or members of a Lutheran academic community—why is the Lutheran Church concerned enough about our context and its consequences to commission this ambitious and sometimes arduous study process? Here are at least some of the reasons:

- Because God created us as beloved creatures, in the image of God, with capacity to know and understand God and the world.

- Because we marvel at and claim our God-given capacities "to communicate, reason, explore new realities, discover meaning and truth, create art, technology and complex societies, enjoy beauty, and discern what is right and good" (*Our Calling in Education*).

- Because God calls us into the vocation of service and responsibility toward our neighbor and in our communities—religious communities built around faith and grace (the heavenly kingdom) and secular communities built around laws and the common good (the earthly kingdom).

- Because historically we have been concerned about education in the faith. One recalls Luther's injunction to families regarding such matters. We are reminded of his energy and leadership in establishing schools so that children and adults would possess the skills necessary to read and interpret the Word. We remember Luther's preparation of educational materials including the large and small catechisms.

- Because Lutherans have been concerned about, and respectful of, human reason and secular knowledge, recognizing them as God's good gifts, gifts that contribute to knowledge of the faith, and as gifts that are essential to our vocations in the world.

- Because Lutherans are committed to civic righteousness, (Augsburg Confession, Article XVI) or to the common good. Luther exemplified this conviction in his own life. One thinks of his commitment to the establishment of the common schools, to the university, to social welfare, to new governance arrangements, and to new social institutions and new laws (Witte). To be sure, Luther's judgment in these matters, as in the case of the peasant's revolt, was not unerring; but his concern for civic righteousness, consistent with his formulation on the two kingdoms, was clear.

- Because we are a people of hope. Freed from the oppressions of "contexts and consequences" by the blood of the cross, we are able to respond to God's call to nurture the young, to care for creation and to love the neighbor. God has given us both experience and resources with which to build meaningful vocations in our lives individually and in the lives of our families, congregations, communities, colleges and universities.

- Finally, we are encouraged to address our calling in education by the signs that we see around us, including education reform in schools, a vast expansion in congregational schools, educational innovation in our colleges and universities, a renewal of mission in higher education, and revitalized youth ministries. There are leaders with vision and expertise who are passionate about the Lutheran calling in education.

Given the looming issues and the resolve to address our calling in education, what are the *prospects and possibilities?* As a foreword to this discussion, let me pause a moment. In good Lutheran tradition, our theologizing and thinking about vocation is grounded in word and sacrament. The word provides grounding, counsel, and revelation, as we seek to discern the will of God for our time and in our station. So let me frame these remarks about prospects and possibilities with these words from Romans. Paul writes: "Do not be conformed to this world but be ye transformed by the renewing of your mind so that you may discern what is the will of God—what is good and acceptable and perfect" (Romans 12:2).

I believe that the Lutheran calling in education is about transformation. I think it is about renewing our minds by acquiring new knowledge, by wrestling with the paradox and ambiguity of the current circumstances in education, and by developing and testing new strategies and insights. It is about discerning the will of God in these matters—a process fed by prayer, faithful study, and honest conversation. In that spirit, I submit some grist for the renewing of our minds —for we have significant resources with which to pursue our calling in education.

In assessing our prospects and possibilities we begin with the legacies: the biblical legacy, the confessional legacy, the theological legacy, and the pedagogical legacy. I have already illustrated the biblical legacy. Now let us consider the *confessional legacy.*

- Earlier I noted references to the first article of the Apostles' Creed. This article affirms our creation in the image of God, the gift of knowledge, and the call to steward God's creation.

- The second article acknowledges the fallenness of creation, the reality of sin, of evil, of the sorts of inequities and injustices identified in the study document.

- But it also establishes the gospel, the transforming capacity of Christ that allows us to transcend our brokenness, to transform life and the world. This is an exercise of the Christian freedom that Luther celebrated.

- The second article is also an account of the gospel, this good news that motivates us to serve God, to love the neighbor, and to engage in the sometimes arduous tasks of being in community.

- It is in the third article that we acknowledge the work of the Holy Spirit in calling us to faith and into community. It is the Holy Spirit that produces in us and in our communities such fruits as love, joy, peace, and kindness.

- Along side the Apostles' Creed stand the Nicene Creed, the Athanasian Creed, the Augsburg Confession, and the Book of Concord—all documents that seek to articulate the faith and its implications. Taken together, they constitute a rich legacy.

Companion to the legacies of word and the confessions stands our *theological legacy*. Luther did not produce a systematic body of theological writings. What we have are his sermons, lectures, prayers, occasional letters, and his Table Talks. Luther was always engaging scripture and reason and people around central questions of life and issues of the community. From this work we deduce a series of theological insights. For example,

- Luther's insights about vocation are central to the enterprise of this annual conference. Luther's understanding was and is distinctive. For Luther, vocation is motivated by gratitude for the good news. It is inclusive of all careers. We are, said Luther, a "priesthood of all believers," so whether cow herder or castle dweller, priest or plumber, teacher or tool maker—all careers provide places of service to the neighbor, places to glorify God in the doing of good work. Further, in Luther's view our vocation is comprehensive of all dimensions of our lives—family, community, church, and career. Luther saw vocation in incarnational terms, in our lives of service to the neighbor we who are finite creatures bare the infinite love of God.

- Luther's teaching about the two kingdoms is another element of his legacy. It provides refreshing insights about our call to work with others in behalf of justice in a world of many faiths and cultures, and it affirms the place of secular knowledge and human reason. "For Lutherans the knowledge given in faith and the knowledge given through human reason are distinct, and both are gifts of God; the two belong together, the one challenging and strengthening the other" (*Our Calling in Education*). And his helpful distinctions between law and gospel provide insights about the error of misplaced piety, the necessity of good laws for our temporal existences, and the freedom of the Christian.

Now we move to Luther's *pedagogical legacy*.

- First of all, this man was committed to learning and to the free, unfettered search for truth. He exemplified St. Anselm's dictum that "faith seeks understanding." It was intellectual inquiry fed by religious anxiety that led Luther to his breakthrough reading of Romans on the nature of salvation. It was Luther's commitment to the laity, the priesthood of all believers, that led him to champion a universal education that would give people of both sexes and all ages direct access to knowledge. It was Luther's commitment to worldly truth that led him to exclaim, "How can you not know what can be known?" It was his respect for human curiosity that led him to write the catechism with its recurrent question, "What does this mean?" It was his commitment to learning in church and world that led Luther and Melanchthon to spearhead a reformation of the curriculum at Wittenberg University.

- The reformation of the curriculum reflected another feature of Luther's pedagogical legacy: his commitment to education in the liberal arts. Luther thought it necessary and appropriate that those who would provide leadership in church and society should be acquainted with history, science, philosophy, and language in order to discover the truth of God's word and the best course of action in the church and community.

- We also celebrate Luther's commitment to excellence in all things. He was alleged by some to have said, "A good cobbler makes good shoes, not poor shoes with little crosses on them." Whether he said it or not, he viewed piety as an unacceptable excuse for mediocrity. No doubt he subscribed to the Apostle Paul's admonitions about running the good race with perseverance.

- Luther's commitment to the dialectic, to the engagement of faith and life, and to moral deliberation about faith and the common good is another aspect of his legacy. He exemplified it in his writing and speaking, he demonstrated it in his Table Talk which addressed both the ordinary and extraordinary experiences of life, and he advocated for the dialectic in the reconstitution of the curriculum of Wittenberg around a more rhetorical, dialogical model of engaged learning.

- A final piece of Luther's pedagogical legacy was his sense of contingency. It is expressed in a number of ways, including the famous *simul justis et peccator* formulation, the confession that we are both sinner and righteous. We also see it in Luther's view on the limits of reason. Luther viewed reason as the "most important and the highest in rank among all things, and, in comparison with other things of this life, the best and something divine." But he was leery of Erasmus and others who thought they could rationalize divine grace and revelation, and he was sensitive to the ways in which persons who were simultaneously saint and sinner could corrupt reason. The sense of contingency is also evident in Luther's preference for the paradoxical, the reality of the sometimes irresolvable tension among alternative ways of understanding and negotiating reality. This sense of contingency leads to a sense of intellectual humility.

Now we move beyond the legacy to another set of observations on the prospects and possibilities for the Lutheran calling in education. A particular sign of encouragement is the renewal of the apostolic paradigm in the church. The work of Loren Meade, Stanley Hauerwas, and William B. Willimon a decade and a half ago described the stagnation of ministry and mission in many churches. They were, in a word, focused on self-preservation and unseen and distant mission activities. But in the fifteen years since the publication of these books, we have seen remarkable movement in many congregations. We see, in particular, a focus on equipping the laity for their ministries in daily life. We see the preparation of pastors for apostolic ministry in a post-Christian world where Christian beliefs and values are not shared by the culture. We see focus on small group ministries that address social needs and spiritual development. We see lively and engaged forms of worship, education, and youth ministry.

Another reason for optimism is the renaissance of Christian colleges. The postmodern consciousness and the secular angst among many of us led to some deep reflection about religious identity and mission on many of our campuses. The result is, in many cases, a revitalized community evidenced by lively conversation about faith and learning and about vocation. New curricular and pedagogical models are surfacing with a powerful assist from the Lilly Endowment. Scholars like Schwehn, Benne, Bunge, Simmons, Christenson, Jodock, and Lagerquist (among others) have provided excellent material for the renewing of our minds and our campuses and our programs. This annual conference, the Lutheran Academy of Scholars and the publication *Intersections*, further testify to the reality of this renaissance. Furthermore, we know that Lutheran colleges and universities make a difference. The data gathered by the Lutheran Educational Conference of North America in its multi-year research program indicates that our institutions excel in educational outcomes related to faith development, in the integration of faith and learning, in opportunities for discussion of faith issues, and in levels of participation in the life of a church following graduation.

We hasten to include on our list of encouraging news items the reform movements in public K-12 education. Upset with the experience of their students and the performance of schools, parents, politicians, and philanthropists are developing alternative formats and platforms. Consequently, vouchers, charter schools, and home schools are now part of our vocabulary. That does not begin to describe the myriad innovations occurring in many schools where teachers and administrators are showing very creative leadership.

I mentioned earlier the response of Lutheran congregations to the educational needs of their members and their neighborhoods. Our study document reports that one in five ELCA congregations is sponsoring some sort of educational venture reaching 225,000 students and engaging 20,000 teachers, administrators, and staff members. Between 1999 and 2004 an average of fifty schools or early childhood centers were opened every year. This ministry is, in all likelihood, our church's most effective venture in reaching an increasingly multicultural population.

Finally, the prospects for our calling in education are enhanced by the quest for values, for virtue, and for meaning that we see exhibited in our society. One thinks of the popularity of books like *The Purpose-Driven Life* or the "Ethics and" movement exemplified at the Hoover Institution where *Fortune* magazine senior writer Marc Gunther led a seminar on "Compassionate Capitalism" and is the author of several books and essays on related subjects. One could cite the growing number of independent Bible study groups that are springing up across the country and across denominational lines.

This set of reflections on the context and prospect for the Lutheran calling in education is necessarily incomplete. These are some of the issues, as I see them, and the resources available to us as we seek to shape our calling. I leave it to you to fill in the empty spaces and then make the connections between our resources and our challenges.

This may or may not be a *kairos* time but it is, I submit, a time of significant opportunity for people committed to the kind of holism in education to which our colleges, universities, and church have a historic commitment.

Luther did not conform to the religious ideologies and practices of his place and time, nor did he conform to the civic practices and ideologies of Saxony. He was transformed by the gospel as it was revealed to him in his studies, in his conversation with others, in the writings of St. Paul, and in the work of the Holy Spirit. In the vocation that followed, he became an agent of transformation in church and society.

It happened in the time of Saul who became the apostle Paul. It happened in the time of Luther who became a reformer in the church, the schools, and society. So why not now? That is what the Lutheran calling in education is all about – transformation. So be it. Amen, so be it.

Works Cited

Nancy T. Ammerman, "Running on Empty," *Christian Century* June 28, 2005).

Thomas Bartlett, "College Students Mix Doubt and Belief in Their Spiritual and Religious Views," *Chronicle of Higher Education* (April 14, 2005).

Robert Bellah and Richard Madson, William M. Sullivan, Ann Swidler, and Steven M. Tipton,.*Habits of the Heart* (Berkeley: University of California, 1985).

Robert Benne, *Quality with Soul* (Grand Rapids, Michigan: Wm. B. Eerdmans Publishing Co., 2001).

Albert Borgman, *Crossing the Postmodern Divide* (Chicago: University of Chicago Press, 1992).

"College Drop Outs," *Context* (May, 2004).

Paul J. Dovre, "Re-examination and Renaissance: Lilly Sponsored Studies at the Turn of the Century," www.resourcingchristianity.org, Louisville Seminary, 2003.

Marilyn J. Harran, ed., *Luther and Learning* (Selingsgrove, Pennsylvania: Susquehanna University Press, 1985).

Stanley Hauerwas and William B. Willimon, *Resident Aliens* (Nashville: Abingdon Press, 1990).

Stephen Haynes, ed., *Professing in the Postmodern Academy: Faculty and the Future of Church Related Colleges* (Waco, Texas: Baylor University Press, 2002).

Richard T. Hughes, *The Vocation of a Christian Scholar: How Christian Faith Can Sustain the Life of the Mind*, revised edition (Grand Rapids, Michigan: Wm. B. Eerdmans Publishing Co., 2005).

Luther's Works, Harold J. Grimm, ed. (Philadelphia: Fortress Press, 1957).

Roland M. Martinson and Tom Beaudin, "Spiritual But Not Religious: Reaching the 'Lost' Generations—Understanding Mission Among 18-30 Year Olds," Hein-Fry Lecture, 2001.

George M. Marsden, *The Soul of the American University: From Protestant Establishment to Established Unbelief* (New York: Oxford University Press, 1994).

Loren Meade, *The Once and Future Church* (Washington, D.C.: The Alban Institute, 1991).

"Media Fellow Marc Gunther Discusses Compassionate Capitalism," *Hoover Institution Newsletter* (Spring, 2005).

Our Calling in Education: A First Draft of a Social Statement, Task Force on Education, Division for Church and Society, Evangelical Lutheran Church in America, 2006.

Our Calling in Education: A Lutheran Study, Task Force on Education, Division for Church and Society, Evangelical Lutheran Church in America, 2004.

Robert D. Putnam, *Bowling Alone: The Collapse and Revival of American Community* (New York: Simon and Schuster, 2000).

Mark Schwehn, *Exiles in Eden: Religion and the Academic Vocation in America* (New York: Oxford University Press, 1993).

Sandra Scofield, Review of *Soul Searching, Chicago Tribune* February 20, 2005).

Ernest L. Simmons, *Lutheran Higher Education: An Introduction for Faculty* (Minneapolis: Augsburg Fortress, 1998).

Douglas Sloan, *Faith and Knowledge: Mainline Protestantism and American Higher Education* (Louisville, Kentucky: Westminster/John Knox, 2002).

Christian Smith and Melinda Lindquist Denton, *Soul Searching: The Religious and Spiritual Lives of American Teenagers* (New York: Oxford University Press, 2005).

Andrea Sterk, ed., *Religious Scholarship and Higher Education: Perspectives and Directions for the Future* South Bend, Indiana: Notre Dame University Press, 2002).

The Augsburg Confession, Article XVI.

The Spiritual Life of College Student,. Higher Education Research Institute, University of California, Los Angeles, 2005.

Rick Warren, *The Purpose-Driven Life.* (Grand Rapids, Michigan: Zondervan, 2002).

John Witte Jr., *Law and Protestantism: The Legal Teachings of the Lutheran Reformation* (Cambridge: Cambridge University Press, 2002).

CHAPTER FOURTEEN

A Lutheran Learning Paradigm

2007

This essay identifies some of the distinctive resources of the Lutheran tradition and the ways in which they inform the learning paradigm of Lutheran colleges. This project is prompted by the recent renewal of interest in such matters among Christian colleges in general and Lutheran colleges in particular. For a variety of reasons, many Lutheran colleges are seeking to recover and extend the distinguishing elements of their religious tradition and identity. In most cases, the faculties are religiously diverse and most, including the Lutherans among them, lack an awareness and understanding of the distinctive elements of the Lutheran tradition. This essay is also motivated by the work of others, especially the volume edited by Richard T. Hughes and William B. Adrian, Models of Christian Higher Education.

The distinctive connections between particular religious traditions and their learning paradigms is evident from a cursory survey: While Roman Catholic colleges vary from one order to another, they maintain a relatively consistent focus on the social teachings of the church as well as the work of the great philosophers and theologians. In addition, one notes the Thomist and neo-Thomist traditions of the Jesuits and the focus on hospitality and service among the Benedictines. The Mennonite schools have a particular focus on the application of Christian ethics and social justice teachings in domestic and international venues of service. There is the rigorous Kyperian tradition among Dutch Reformed schools with their emphasis on the formulation of a Christian worldview, discipline by discipline, leading to a true integration of faith and learning.

The Hughes and Adrian book was published in 1997. The editors and other contributors characterized, and distinguished among, various learning models (or paradigms) in religious higher education. They noted that Lutherans, out of their culture-affirming, two kingdoms dialectical construct, typically seek to establish a dialogue between the Christian vision and the world. Out of their sacramental tradition, Roman Catholic schools seek to bring the presence of Christ into a world in need. On the other hand, out of their convictions about the sovereignty of God, schools in the Reformed tradition seek to approach every discipline from a distinctive Christian perspective. In cryptic expression, schools in the Reformed tradition seek to transform learning by bringing it under the sovereignty of God, Lutherans seek an engagement between faith and learning, and Roman Catholic institutions seek to integrate a Christian vision into the life of the academy. Spurred by the work of Hughes, Adrian, and others, I think it is useful to explore in more detail the resources inherent in the Lutheran tradition and the ways in which they might conceivably shape the learning paradigm—that is, both the program of learning and its execution.

The work of others shapes this paper in a number of ways. In addition to the works of Luther and the Lutheran Confessions, I have been informed most recently by the work of five contemporary scholars. They are Ernest Simmons, Darrell Jodock, Tom Christenson, Robert Benne, and Richard Hughes. In his text designed to introduce faculty to the Lutheran tradition in higher education, Simmons sketches out the history of Lutheran higher education and mines the theological lode of Lutheranism. He identifies the doctrines of justification and the incarnation as formative as well as the Lutheran distinction between law and gospel and the Lutheran teachings on vocation. He describes the Lutheran notion that we are simultaneously saint and sinner, unable to escape human temptation yet capable of righteous acts. He cites the work of K. Glen Johnson describing the Lutheran penchant for paradox and the "tension-filled distinctions such as law and gospel, faith and works, saint and sinner, finite versus infinite, reason and faith."

Simmons gives extensive treatment to the notion of vocation as does his friend and colleague, Darrell Jodock. Jodock has written frequently and lectured widely on Lutheran higher education. He places vocation in a Lutheran context and sees it as a response to the grace of God that is lived out in service to our neighbor and the world and for the sake of the common good. Vocation is lived out in the home, church, career, and community; it is inclusive of all honorable callings, both secular and sacred. Drawing on the Lutheran understanding of human nature, living out one's vocation involves struggle, ambiguity, and change. For that reason among others, we live out our vocation with others, that is, in community where together we test ideas, share wisdom, and seek divine guidance. As Jodock and other writers note, Lutherans stand in a tradition of encouraging diligent study in preparation for the living out of vocation in the world. With the encouragement and assistance of the Lilly Endowment, vocation has become a widely employed tool for centering and focusing Christian higher education.

In his well-read book, *Quality with Soul,* Robert Benne identifies three defining themes in the Lutheran theological tradition including a strong emphasis on the confessions and confessionally trained pastors, the emphasis on calling or vocation, and the affirmation of "human reason as a guide to earthly, civil life." For Benne, the Christian account of reality should give vision, direction, and content to the academic enterprise of a Christian college in intentional, self-conscious ways. It should be embedded in the faculty and staff, in the course of study, and in the ethos of the community. Benne's assessment of St. Olaf College and Valparaiso University illustrate the dynamics of his template.

A fourth contemporary resource is Tom Christenson and his *The Gift and Promise of Lutheran Higher Education.* In this book Christenson takes into account the significant changes in the Christian academy and seeks to tell the Lutheran story using both new and familiar categories of thought. He is committed to the Lutheran idea of vocation as an organizing principal. He identifies eight theological theses inherent in the Lutheran tradition with fresh language and engaging illustrations. One of the other unique contributions of his book is his discussion of the constituents and dynamics of a Lutheran epistemology. He goes on to identify some of the implications of the Lutheran gift in the formation of the curriculum and its pedagogy.

Especially interesting is the work of Richard Hughes. What makes it interesting is both his perspective as an outsider from the Lutheran tradition and his assessment of both the strengths and weaknesses of our theological resources. He identifies our key resources as Luther's insistence on human finitude, the sovereignty of God, and the notion of paradox that is embedded in Luther's theology of the cross and is expressed in his notion of the two kingdoms. Hughes has great confidence in this tradition to keep questions alive, to live with complexity, to avoid the dogmatic, and to deal with the limits to human understanding gracefully. He also warns of the temptation of paradox thinking to fall off one side or another of the paradox or, alternately, to surrender to a relativism.

To conclude this survey, I note again that my task is to draw on these several insights about the Lutheran tradition in sketching a Lutheran learning paradigm and its implications for both the content and pedagogy of the curriculum. To be sure, while this is the sort of thing that people in, for example, the Dutch Reformed tradition do with discipline and regularity, it is not the sort of thing Lutherans have done for a variety of reasons. So, in providing this sketch, I mean to be helpful by providing a template and not a formula, a list of possibilities and not a fixed plan. I do so knowing that Lutheran college faculties will, in any case, make their own best judgment on these matters.

So to the task at hand: I submit that the Lutheran tradition is shaped by four narratives: the biblical, the confessional, the theological, and the vocational.

Luther was an Old Testament scholar and the *biblical* story was the bedrock of his preaching, teaching, and leadership. Most of his published work was about biblical resources. He came at his theology, never systematized, out of his biblical work for the most part. For Luther, "Word alone, grace alone, faith alone" starts there.

The Lutheran *confessional* narrative was shaped by many church leaders over the centuries. It includes the classical creeds of the church including the Apostles', the Nicean, and the Athanasian Creeds, as well as the Augsburg Confession. Each was an attempt to express biblical truths in relationship to the believer and the world. These confessions provide Christians with a paradigm for understanding themselves in relationship to God and the world. Inspired by God's

Spirit and created by God's people, they are subject to interpretation and reconsideration from age to age. But over the centuries they have proven durable and useful guides to the Christian life.

Lutherans do not claim a unique *theological* system, but they do affirm the importance of the human quest to understand the implications of God's revelation for the lives of God's people in the world. Lutherans have sought out and affirmed theological work from many traditions. With strong grounding in the scholastic, pietistic, and critical traditions, Lutherans have been in the first rank of the world's theologians. Lutherans bring to the ecumenical theological conversation certain distinctive motifs including most notably the two kingdoms, the priesthood of all believers, original sin, the theology of the cross, *simul justis et peccator*, the incarnation, and its teaching on justification. Imbedded in the Lutheran theological tradition are some pedagogical proclivities including the dialectic, the paradoxical, the commitment to moral deliberation, and freedom of inquiry. As exemplified by Luther's theology of the cross, "there is a persistent warning . . . to avoid the facile, the simplistic—to offer easy religious answers to human questions." (Hall)

The *vocational narrative* is also distinctive in the Lutheran tradition. Luther's passion for the priesthood of all believers, his commitment to love the neighbor, and his sense that all areas of life are avenues for the expression of our love for God constitute substantive elements of the Lutheran vocational narrative. For Luther, vocation was not to be equated with a career or a job or the calling to a holy order. Rather, our vocation comes to us in baptism and is lived out in joyful response to God's gift of love. God frees us to love our neighbor and promote the common good in all of our places of responsibility in daily life—home, congregation, work place, neighborhood, nation, and global society. For Lutherans, vocation is where God's gift and call come together in the concreteness, the humus, of life. In this context, the purpose of Lutheran higher education is to prepare students for vocation, with all that implies.

So if these are the key narratives, what might a Lutheran learning paradigm look like and what would be its implications for curricula and the pedagogical design of academic programs in Lutheran colleges? First of all, the aim of a Lutheran paradigm of learning is the engagement of faith and the secular disciplines. Consistent with its two kingdoms framework and its respect for the secular disciplines of the academy, Lutherans seek to discover what the propositions of faith have to contribute to secular disciplines and vice versa. Since God is a transcendent reality, knowledge of the faith and knowledge of the world is all from God and all about God.

Now in light of the goal and nature of the learning paradigm, what about the curriculum? In view of the centrality of the biblical narrative, the study of sacred scriptures will be *de rigor* in the curriculum. The objective here is both knowledge of the story and knowing how to read it for oneself. This kind of knowledge will be of value to all persons, Christian and other, since it is a cultural and world shaping literature. Given the dismal state of biblical literacy in a world of many faiths and cultures, one could give special priority to this matter in the modern age, especially at Lutheran places.

Studies in theology will be another explicit element in the curriculum. These courses will set up and address both the big issues of meaning and the ordinary issues of living. The study of theology comes in many forms from history to systematic theology to confessional theology to ethics. What used to be thought of as the sole province of professional theologians is now claimed by practitioners in a variety of academic disciplines (e.g. ethics and business, ethics and science, ethics and communication, etc) for the Word has something to do with everything and everyone, and theologians are not the only players in this arena. However, at Lutheran schools it would be most desirable to see theologians involved as partners in the "and" curricula.

It is anticipated that the Lutheran confessional narrative may be nested in both the study of scripture and the study of theology. The confessions provide evidence of the way in which human beings have come to understand the truths of the scripture and the continuing revelation of God. They answer the perennial Lutheran question: "What does this mean?" Such questions are especially germane in the lives of the millennial generation that seeks both significance and status.

The vocational narrative is receiving growing attention in Lutheran and other Christian colleges in America. This development reflects both a response to the initiatives of the Lilly Endowment and the reclaiming of a central theological theme. Not many places will establish courses devoted solely to vocation. Rather, the idea of our calling to vocation underlies the whole academic project at Lutheran places. It becomes foundational for the whole enterprise. But the groundwork, the building blocks, must be established and then reiterated throughout the college years. Some schools introduce the idea in the orientation of new students, others include it as an explicit consideration in one or another core courses (sometimes in religion).

Closely related to the unfolding of the Lutheran idea of vocation is the call to serve the neighbor, the common good. Again, in recent years we have seen the advent of service learning in which theory is integrated with practice. In this way, the curriculum, service to the neighbor, and the advancement of the common good are of a piece. Lutheran schools are in a unique position in that they may bring to this form of applied learning the rationale of our theological tradition and thus value is added to the experience.

In what ways might the Lutheran tradition inform pedagogical practices? Luther exemplified moral deliberation in his life, ministry, and scholarship. He was especially committed to, and confident in, the moral deliberation of the community. He would say, in effect: "Here is what scripture says and here is the situation we face, so what shall we do?" He felt such deliberation was necessary both because there were not always clear answers in scripture to every situation and because human beings, by nature, distort reality. So he believed deliberation, the give and take of the community, was needed. Luther did not always get it right and he knew that, but he believed in the power of the Spirit working among the people of God as they sought practical solutions in both material and churchly matters. He also had confidence that in graciousness God would forgive the mistakes. All of which suggests that Lutheran places will, explicitly and self consciously, be places of moral deliberation in which faculty serve as models and students are engaged in the discernment of wisdom.

Closely related to moral deliberation is the dialectic. Dialectic, or dialogue, may be a solo activity or a communal activity. We often speak about the dialogue between faith and learning wherein we attempt to discover what the truth of faith has to contribute to our understanding of a body of knowledge and what that body of knowledge can contribute to our understanding of faith. Such conversation is tinged with the realism of ambiguity, of not knowing all there is to know, of sometimes coming out in the wrong place. Thus there is a necessary humility about it. Mistakes in human judgment and the humility those mistakes engender are among the reasons that many Lutherans (and Protestants) have tended toward quietism and retreat in the face of the inscrutable or imponderable or the merely controversial. But that historic fact is not an excuse for inaction. Indeed, Luther was quite aware of these problems and, in spite of them and in view of God's grace, encouraged his followers to "sin boldly."

This approach I have described necessitates a strong faculty commitment to, and literacy about, the tradition I have described. It also implies that the religion faculty will carry a college wide responsibility for instruction in the Lutheran biblical and theological tradition. While there will be some specific courses dedicated to particular areas of narrative content (e.g. Bible, church history, theology, etc.), the implementation of the tradition must reach to all elements of the curriculum, for each provides an opportunity for dialectic, all provide venues for vocational reflection, and many provide challenges in moral discernment. Some schools are introducing the underlying learning paradigm of the school in early course work, reinforcing key ideas strategically throughout the college experience and then seeking a comprehensive integration in the form of a capstone course on the eve of graduation.

In an examination of the resources of various religious traditions, Richard T. Hughes observes that "the Lutheran tradition possesses some of the most potent theological resources for sustaining the life of the mind that one can imagine." So while the Lutheran tradition, filled with ambiguities and paradox, is a challenging one to grasp and live out in the academy, it is buttressed by an account of reality that is full of hope. It is a tradition that is appropriate to a world that is both wonder-full and broken.

Works Cited

Robert Benne, *Quality with Soul* (Grand Rapids, Michigan: Wm. B. Eerdmans Publishing Co., 2001).

Tom Christenson, *The Gift and Task of Lutheran Higher Education* (Minneapolis: Augsburg Fortress, 2004).

Douglas John Hall, *The Cross in Our Context* (Minneapolis: Fortress Press, 2003).

Richard T. Hughes and William B. Adrian, *Models of Christian Higher Education* (Grand Rapids, Michigan: Wm. B. Eerdmans Publishing Co., 1997).

Richard T. Hughes, *How Christian Faith Can Sustain the Life of the Mind.* (Grand Rapids, Michigan: Wm. B. Eerdmans Publishing Co., 2001).

Darrell Jodock, "Freedom, Humor, and Community: A Lutheran Vision of Higher Education," *Intersections*, No. 13 (Winter, 2002).

Darrell Jodock, "The Lutheran Tradition and the Liberal Arts," *Called to Serve: St. Olaf College and the Vocation of a Church College*, Pamela Schwandt, ed. (Northfield, Minnesota: St. Olaf College, 1999).

Darrell Jodock, Unpublished lectures, Thrivent Fellows Leadership Development Program, 2002-2005.

Martin Luther, "The Christian in Society," *Luther's Works*, Volume 45, Walther I. Brandt, ed., Helmut T. Lehman, general editor (Philadelphia: Fortress Press, 1962).

Ernest L. Simmons, *Lutheran Higher Education: An Introduction for Faculty* (Minneapolis: Augsburg Fortress, 1998).

CHAPTER FIFTEEN

Lutheran Colleges: Past and Prologue

2009

My association with Lutheran higher education dates back to 1952 when I enrolled at Concordia College in Moorhead, Minnesota. Since then, with the exception of just six years, I have been involved in Lutheran higher education as a student, teacher, dean, president, and consultant. In response to invitations from others and my interest in the history of Lutheran colleges, I will share my perceptions on several of the key trends that have character ized the past fifty years in the history of Midwestern Lutheran colleges. In both method and content, this should be regarded as autobiographical rather than academic, for it is more about reminiscence than research.

As the template for the historical assessments that follow, I draw from the classical sources of persuasion as identified by Aristotle and others. According to the classics, people are persuaded or convinced by three distinctive sources or proofs: ethos, logos, and pathos.

Ethos is the power of one's personality, character, and reputation. We say we are convinced because the person making the argument is deemed to be honest, trustworthy, knowledgeable, or loyal. I think that organizations and institutions have *ethos* as well, and it is derived from their mission, their values, their traditions, and their character. The *ethos* of a college is transmitted through the people who consti tute the institution, primarily the faculty and staff.

Logos is the second source of persuasion and it has to do with arguments and evidence—that is to say, with logic. When we say that a speech was substantive and persuasive, it means that we were con vinced by the arguments and supporting evidence the speaker was able to offer. I believe institutions have a *logos* in that they make a case for what they stand for or what they have to offer their constituents. If they present well-formed arguments and supporting evidence, good programs and sound learning, they are both respected and understood.

Finally, *pathos* is a form of persuasion that appeals to our wants, desires, or emotions. Such persuasion may appeal to either our basic instincts or our higher inclinations. Institutions also offer *pathos* to their constituents as they appeal to ideals, values, aspirations, fears, hopes, and even dreams. To the extent that people are inspired by, or in congruence with, these elements they will be content, moved, or even inspired.

In my view, at mid-twentieth century, Midwestern Lutheran colleges made their case to their constituents of faculty, staff, alumni, church members, friends, and students primarily on the basis of *pathos* and *ethos*. These colleges were generally places of unity and common focus, shaped by religious and ethnic identity and a strong sense of shared values and commitments. With the passing of the generations and the presence of a more diverse faculty and a more secular and pluralistic culture, both the *pathos* and *ethos* declined in their efficacy. Many new faculty "knew not Joseph," and so the traditions, values, and general character of these places did not have a strong impact on them. Toward the end of the century, spurred on by serious self-examination and growing numbers of inquiring faculty and the support of the church, *logos* became the focus and the basis for institutional renewal. I believe that this emerging *logos* is having a significant impact upon these institutions.

As a way of explicating these matters, let me share my perceptions about the church and Midwestern Lutheran colleges during this period of change. The church was a major part of the context within which these colleges carried out their mission during the past half century. There have been substantial changes in the church's experience, and those changes have had an impact in the life of the schools. For example, the church has changed from a mono-ethnic institution growing from within to a multiethnic church depending on outreach for growth. At a different pace perhaps, the schools have experienced a similar trend toward greater diversity in the ethnic, religious, and economic (if not racial) backgrounds of students, faculty, and staff. In similar fashion, the church has made the transition from being insular to being energetically ecumenical. Mirroring this, the colleges have attracted students from a broad ecumenical spectrum. The church has changed from a body fairly clear about positions on moral and ethical issues to a church that is full of divisions over such matters. While the colleges may not have experienced such divisions in the ways that the church has, they are clearly places with a diversity of opinion and a liberal bias in such matters. At mid-century the church was a major collecting and distribution point for benevolence dollars, and the colleges enjoyed high priority in that distribution. By century's end, benevolence dollars were scarce and the colleges, thought to be able to fend more or less on their own financially, were much lower on the priority list. Somewhat shadowing this development, a church that at mid-century paid close attention to its schools and held them accountable in a number of ways, now has both less time for, and less claim upon, such accountability.

A second template identifies four key issues around which I will discuss developments in the five decades of the second half of the twentieth century. Those key issues are survival, respectability, faithfulness, and relationship to the church. In the 1950s the leaders of the Midwestern colleges were Stavig at Augustana, Christianson at Augsburg, Carlson at Gustavus, Ylvisaker at Luther, Becker at Wartburg, Granskou at St. Olaf, and Knutson at Concordia. All except Carlson had ministerial preparation and parish experience. All were active leaders in their respective church bodies, and these men gave leadership at a time when institutional authority was more centered in the office of the president than at any time since then.

Of the key issues, survival was the one that occupied most of the attention of these colleges. These were the post-Depression, post-WWII days when campus infrastructures were run down, facilities were totally inadequate for the expanding growth caused by returning veterans, and there were not enough qualified faculty to cover all of the classes. Lutheran colleges were not unique in these regards; their state was the common state of most of higher education. A piece of good news was that, although the faculty was stretched thin, there were among them some giants who defined the quality and character of these institutions. The second issue was respectability. Most of higher education had been given a pass on rising academic standards during the survival years of the 1930s and 1940s. But in the post war the accrediting bodies began to flex their muscles. There was pressure to add Ph.D.s to the faculty, to improve library holdings, and to provide adequate equipment and facilities, particularly in the sciences.

With respect to the third key issue, faithfulness, the story is rather straightforward: Each college was a monoculture of the sponsoring church body; almost all of the faculty and staff were Lutheran as well as most of the students. In most cases attendance was required at daily chapel, and the religion requirement consisted of several classes taken over four years. Campus rules and norms reflected the culture and expectations of the church. The mission identity of these colleges was not a matter discussed very often; it could simply be taken for granted. The *ethos* and *logos* of these places was not very self-conscious, but it was constitutive; one can only wonder how these institutions could have prevailed through times of testing without this reality. As a contribution to the *logos* of these institutions, the Lutheran College Faculty group undertook a decade-long study that resulted in the publication of *Christian Faith and the Liberal Arts,* which examined the theological underpinnings of a Lutheran college and their implications for the curriculum. With respect to the church relationship, there was a strong tie. The financial support of the church body was a significant variable in the financial well-being of each school. The church kept a close and loving eye on these colleges. The presidents were, without exception, also church leaders. The governance relationship between the church and the colleges was very strong; in most cases, church leaders had places on the governing boards and every board member was a member of the sponsoring church. Governing boards paid more attention to the details of managing the colleges, a practice grown out of the necessities of the 1930s and 1940s.

The decades of the 1960s and 1970s were marked by leadership changes at many of the colleges; from Stavig to Balcer at Augustana, from Christianson to Anderson at Augsburg, from Ylvisaker to Farwell at Luther, from Carlson to Barth at Gustavus, from Becker to Bachman at Wartburg, from Granskou to Rand at St. Olaf, and from Knutson to Dovre at Concordia toward the end of that period.

It should be noted that, in several cases, the new leaders brought stronger academic credentials and often less theological education. This was the case at Augustana, Luther, Wartburg, Gustavus, and Concordia. With respect to the defining issues, while material survival was not in question, there was significant financial pressure related to expanding and improving campus facilities and providing necessary financial assistance to students. Federal policies and resources turned out to be of immense importance in meeting these needs with the advent of loans and grants for students, loans for building student housing, and loans and grants for improving academic facilities. On several campuses there were construction projects underway every year for twenty years in succession. Since loans had to be repaid and grants did not cover all of the construction costs, each of the colleges put additional resources into fundraising with good results. Alumni, church members, and community friends were committed to these schools, and their generosity followed.

During these decades the schools grew in academic respectability. Faculty numbers increased, and the percentages of faculty with Ph.D.s increased as well, all of which was very important to accreditation agencies. New programs were initiated on every campus, and library and laboratory facilities were upgraded. Faithfulness to mission and tradition became more challenging during this period of time for a number of reasons. Increasingly and with pressure for academic respectability and shortages of personnel, faculty appointments were likely to place more emphasis on academic qualifications than other factors. Most of the new academics came from research centers in which they had been shaped by modernism that placed priority on scientific methods of establishing truth claims. This trend, in turn, placed pressure on the humanities and the religious values that were intrinsic to the distinctiveness of the schools. Curriculum changes tended to diminish the size of the religion requirement. Chapel attendance was by now voluntary but still substantial. The advent of the civil rights movement and the anti-war movement led to myriad changes in the society and its institutions. Some of those changes (e.g., more diverse faculty and student bodies) had a positive impact on the colleges while others (destructive lifestyles) did not. Two of the consequences were the increasing secularization of the schools and the demise of *in loco parentis*.

As it had in the 1950s, The Association of Lutheran College Faculties was minding the *logos* of Lutheran colleges, addressing both the rapidly changing culture of the late 1960s and 1970s and the challenges for Lutheran colleges. The association's work led to the publication of *The Quest for a Viable Saga* by Richard Baepler and others in 1977. The American Lutheran Church initiated the Theological Development Program for Faculty in the 1970s, a program that helped shape a number of persons who would emerge as faculty and administrative leaders in the 1980s and 1990s. However, in most instances, the attention given to institutional mission (*logos*) by most colleges in the 1960s and 1970s was of a lower priority than the attention given to institutional quality. The discussions of mission rarely gave systematic attention to the ways in which the mission might impact the academic life. However, in most cases faculty leaders were persons who had come in the 1940s and 1950s and were infused with the *pathos* and *ethos* of which I wrote earlier.

There were several emerging trends in these decades with respect to the colleges' relationship to the church. To begin with, while church support was still a stable and growing part of the church budgets, reflecting the continuing priority of the colleges, church benevolence declined substantially as a percentage of the rapidly growing budgets of the colleges. Another marked trend in this period was the growing generosity of individual church members with respect to the financial needs of the colleges. In the case of the American Lutheran Church, a major churchwide campaign was very successful. During the 1970s some Lutheran colleges revised their governing documents to include non-Lutheran members. This reflected the growing ecumenism of both the church and the colleges as well as the desire to "spread a bigger net" in search of influence, financial support, and enrollment. In the Lutheran Church in America, colleges developed covenants with synods in their regions as a way of setting forth the mutual commitments that would guide the relationships. It is accurate to say that, with respect to Midwestern Lutheran colleges, college presidents were still thought of as prominent in the leadership of the church.

The decade of the 1980s saw a myriad of leadership changes in these colleges: At Augsburg College Oscar Anderson was succeeded by Charles Anderson; Augustana moved from Charles Balcer to Bill Nelson and then to Lloyd Svendsbye; St. Olaf from Sidney Rand to Harland Foss and Mel George; Luther from Elwin Farwell to H. George Anderson; Wartburg from William Jellema to Robert Vogel; and Gustavus from Ed Lindell to John Kendall. In all but one case, the new presidents came from academic backgrounds. While finance is always an issue for private colleges, financial survival was not a defining issue in the 1980s. Federal and state financial aid programs were very helpful in maintaining vigorous enrollment. Many of the schools launched and completed sophisticated and successful fund raising programs. In terms of academic quality, the Lutheran colleges were respected by the public. It was during this decade that various national rankings of colleges first appeared, and Midwestern Lutheran colleges earned high ratings. These ratings reflected the academic quality that had been built in the faculty and the attention that was being given to strong academic programs.

Perhaps the most challenging issue in the 1980s was faithfulness to the tradition and mission. By the 1980s the academy was shaped by the Enlightenment focus on knowledge as opposed to learning, and the pedagogy of the scientific method held sway. These developments have been chronicled by George Marsden (*The Soul of the American University*), Douglas Sloan (*Faith and Knowledge*), and Mark Schwehn (*Exiles from Eden*) with respect to the academy in general and by James Burtchaell (*The Dying of the Light*) and Robert Benne (*Quality with Soul*) with respect to religious colleges. The consequences of these trends were to diminish confidence in religious knowledge and the role of faith in the life of the school. Augmented by the reality that secular values were shaping the culture, these trends were real sources of stress for most religious colleges, including Lutheran colleges in the Midwest.

In addition to the growing secularity of the schools, there was more religious diversity on the campuses in the faculty, staff, and student body. While most of the faculty in the 1950s and even into the 1960s had come through the Lutheran pipeline, the majority of appointees in the 1970s and 1980s did not. That meant that the *ethos*, which had been carried in the DNA of the faculty in the 50s, 60s, and 70s, could not be counted upon to carry the tradition in the 80s, and matters of mission could no longer be taken for granted. While in the past academic criteria and institutional/missional fit were held in balance in the faculty selection process, by the 1980s academic criteria held sway. A related shift in the profile of incoming faculty in the 70s and 80s is that they had been shaped in ways that meant their primary allegiance was to their discipline and department rather than to the institution they served. I do not think this was a self-conscious commitment on the part of most people, but it was nonetheless a growing reality. The consequence was a diminished religious *ethos* and *pathos*. During these decades one noted subtle changes in the rhetoric of many colleges with a growing emphasis on academic distinctiveness and a softening in the emphasis on religious identity and mission. This was in some measure due to the fact that Lutheran schools were attracting an increasing number of students from other religious traditions whom they did not want to offend.

The connection between the colleges and the church also changed in the 1980s. The college presidents were less likely to be church leaders. The church was stressed for resources, and hence the financial support for colleges diminished. While Lutheran colleges were included in the mission circle of the newly formed Evangelical Lutheran Church in America (ELCA), they were less central to that mission. The implication of these developments in the church meant that the colleges would assume a larger role in defining the ways and extent to which they would embrace their relationship to the church and mission identity. While it was clearly not the case that any of the Midwestern colleges were hostile to their Lutheran identity or trying to distance themselves from their mission, the close of the 1980s became a kind of watershed for these colleges: The relationship to the church had changed, the self-understanding of these schools as institutions of the church had eroded, and the faculties were not always "at home" in the academic communities of the Lutheran church. In short, the *ethos* that had been carried by an earlier generation had largely disappeared with their retirement, the *pathos* was less clear and compelling, and the *logos* of the Lutheran academic tradition was not a significant factor.

Enter the 1990s: There were myriad changes in leadership: Frame was leading Augsburg, Wagner and Halvorson led Augustana,

Baker and then Torgerson came to Luther, Edwards served at St. Olaf, and Steuer at Gustavus. All of these leaders had academic backgrounds and represented a new generation. Most of them were intrigued by the questions of relationship, identity, and mission, and they came to these conversations with a refreshing curiosity. They were leading healthy schools. While some were more robust from a financial view than others, all were viable; while some had more success in attracting students than others, all had stable numbers. Academically, these schools each continued to make one or more list of best colleges. There were centers of excellence on each campus reflecting the quality and ingenuity of the faculty. A challenge dating from the 1980s was around the "vocationalism" that was sweeping the country. From grade school on students were being pressed to pick a career and pursue a professionally-oriented education. This was a special concern to colleges with a strong liberal arts tradition.

Viewed through the lens of faithfulness to the Lutheran tradition, the 1990s were years of renaissance. The roots of this renaissance were both external and internal. There was a heightened awareness of a values crisis in the society. At the same time, there was an emerging spirituality among the young. In the academy, the postmodern movement provided a critique of modernism, rationalism, and the scientific method. Along with a new generation of leaders came a new generation of faculty members who had, in part, been shaped by this critique, young people who were curious about religious matters and college identity, open to deep conversation about value, meaning, and faith. Providing counsel and leadership were some key faculty and administrative leaders who were schooled in the *logos* of Lutheran higher education.

Out of this crucible of change, religious colleges found both incentive and support for a new self-examination of mission and identity. Many Midwestern Lutheran colleges initiated formal discussions about the meaning and implications of their mission and identity as Lutheran schools. The ELCA supported these efforts with annual conferences on the vocation of Lutheran colleges. These conferences were (and are) well attended and led to the publication of *Intersections*, a journal that features essays about faith and learning. The Lilly Endowment, sensing the new opening for such matters, launched a mammoth program enabling many colleges to initiate comprehensive programs centered on the Christian idea of vocation. Most of the Midwestern Lutheran colleges participated in the program. The ELCA initiated the Lutheran Academy of Scholars, where faculty members could devote themselves to a serious intellectual engagement between faith and learning. Endowed professorships were created on a number of campuses in support of academic endeavor informed by faith commitments. A number of curriculum projects emerged, and for many the touchstone was institutional mission. The Lutheran Educational Conference of North America (LECNA) launched a major research effort designed to identify the unique impact of Lutheran colleges upon their graduates.

To return to the template of *ethos, pathos, and logos*, what happened in the 1990s was the beginning of the reconstruction of a *logos* in behalf of the mission of Lutheran colleges. Mirroring the leadership of their predecessors in the 1950s and 1970s, faculty members examined the Lutheran confessional, academic, and intellectual traditions and found a trove of helpful propositions upon which to build an understanding of both personal and institutional callings. This *logos* is compelling enough to generate conviction, yes even passion, for the cause. Thus we have the re-energizing of the *pathos* of these institutions and, over time, an emerging community *ethos* as well. This is not to suggest that questions about mission and identity are now settled. Indeed, that would defy the Lutheran tradition that is almost constantly in motion about such matters. As the society changes around these schools, the task of reinterpretation must go on.

To complete this historical template, we must consider the relationship of the colleges to the church starting in 2000. Financial support continued to decline in 2000 as churchwide resources grew scarce and the fiscal well-being of most of the colleges made their need less compelling. The ELCA went through a reorganization in which higher education was joined with theological education. While churchwide direct financial support continued to decline, the ELCA continued to sponsor staff development and faculty interchanges in a variety of forums. What is remarkable among the Midwestern Lutheran colleges is the leadership that the presidents have provided in initiating and supporting partnerships with other institutions and agencies of the church.

Out of a vision of unity in mission and interconnectedness in ministry, a number of partnerships are emerging.

In summary, survival was the issue defining the 1950s, respectability was the compelling issue of the 1960s and 1970s, and faithfulness to Lutheran identity and mission emerged in the late 1980s and continues into the current decade. Over the span of the five decades, the relationship with the church evolved from dependence to independence to partnership. The profile of the presidents transitioned from churchly to academic; the cultural inclinations moved from sectarian to secular; the intellectual paradigm shifted from pre-modern, to modern, to postmodern; and the demographic profile moved from homogeneity to a growing diversity. Entering the new century, Midwestern Lutheran colleges enjoyed regional and national reputations for excellence and possessed a robust attitude about their viability. Leaders of excellence mediate complex and stressful institutional agendas in a time of material uncertainty and cultural change. The case for Lutheran colleges, once resting on strong *ethos* and *pathos*, is being reconstructed around a lively and rich *logos*.

What then of the future of these colleges as expressions of the Lutheran tradition in higher education? Perhaps the most obvious answer is that, given the significant autonomy that characterizes Lutheran colleges, they will evolve in unique ways. Given the evolution that has occurred in the past decades, the colleges themselves will be primary in defining their relationship to the church. Setting these matters aside, let me identify a set of key variables in shaping the identity and mission of Lutheran colleges.

The first variable is the student marketplace. It is very difficult to characterize the rising generations of college students; they are at once liberal and conservative, religious and secular, spiritual but not necessarily religious, and materialistic but committed to social action. Clearly, this profile suggests many vantage points for engaging with students around religious matters. We can be reasonably confident that they will come from the full range of religious persuasions including non-Christian traditions, and so colleges will continue to make adjustments, curricular and pedagogical, to that reality. While Lutherans will perhaps remain the largest cohort group in the Midwestern schools, they will not always be in the majority. While these products of postmodernism are interested in the spiritual side of things, they are poorly informed with respect to confessional, theological, and biblical matters. This presents a special challenge and opportunity to those who teach religion. In addition, today's students are not great worship attendees, so campus ministry leaders will face a continuing challenge in the engagement of students in corporate religious practices. These students are close to their parents, sometimes called the "hovering" generation. Cell phones and instant messaging mean that students are always networking, and parents tend to be a significant part of their life experience. Colleges will continue to find their way in adapting to this reality, which presents both opportunity and obstacle.

Another set of variables informing the status of these colleges in relationship to their mission and identity evolves around the faculty. Faculty recruitment will be especially crucial, for faculty more than anyone else must represent and affect the mission of the college. Each college has the right to ask and expect that faculty members from any faith tradition will uphold the mission of the college. While the exegesis of that mission is always a work in progress, colleges should recruit people who are willing to engage that dialogue in a constructive and sympathetic way. Discussion of these expectations should be part of the recruitment and screening process.

For many reasons, the formation of the faculty *ethos* will be of high importance. The faculties are and will be composed of a significant number of persons from non-Christian and non-Lutheran traditions. The presence of this kind of diversity presents both opportunity and challenge—the opportunity (and need) for dialogue (a Lutheran staple) and the challenge of educating those from other traditions. In reflecting on this diversity, Darrell Jodock put it this way:

> In order for these colleges to retain the advantages of
> a tradition that challenges them to be more deeply
> and more profoundly what they already aspire to be,
> the tradition needs to be articulated more clearly and
> affirmed more intentionally.

Since persons entering the professoriate in recent years have been oriented around disciplinary identity rather than institutional identity, there will be a continuing challenge for Lutheran colleges to integrate these persons into the community and engage them in the activities that give life to it. As noted earlier, the postmodern consciousness of faculty educated in the later part of the last century and the early years of this century may be an asset to these schools. The typical postmodernist recognizes the legitimate place of religion in intellectual discourse, is open to the spiritual dimension of their own being, and respects the important role of context or community in framing one's perception and life practice.

Faculty are not the only element in the human variable of course. One thinks about the important roles of presidents, other college leaders, regents, and staff. Leaders of experience and informed commitment to the Lutheran project in education are scarce, so continuing attention to leader identification and development will be essential. The colleges will want to be self-conscious in filling leadership positions with people who share the vision and mission of Lutheran colleges. The influence of persons who are either ill-informed or indifferent to such matters has been, and will be, detrimental to Lutheran schools. Of almost equal importance to the selection of such individuals is the provision of continuing education experiences around mission and identity. Again, if board and staff development around these issues is only left to chance, the results are likely to drift, and such matters would be of growing indifference.

Another variable, perhaps the most important, centers on how we navigate the identity/diversity paradox. We acknowledge the value of both identity and diversity, but have tended in recent years to give the greater weight to diversity. This is perhaps not surprising for institutions that were monocultural in the recent past (and defensive about it) and are well informed about, and widely influenced by, the diversity movement in higher education. It is also to be expected of Lutheran colleges that are, by tradition, culturally engaged institutions. The challenge will be achieving a relationship between these two powerful variables that will be consonant with the mission and identity of a Lutheran college. I think that multiculturalism becomes an asset when the cultures that inform it are well represented. That is, one of the special gifts that Lutheran colleges have to contribute to the multiculture that is our world is a substantive, high quality, and unapologetic representation of the Lutheran and Christian traditions.

In other words, this identity becomes an asset, something to build on and never be apologetic about. Of course I am not arguing for some new parochialism but for a hearty multiculturalism that draws special strength from what the Lutheran tradition brings to it. One of those strengths is a commitment to engage in conversation with other faith traditions and to literally "test all things," including our own tradition. This view of the identity/diversity paradox underscores earlier comments about the importance of recruiting faculty for mission and providing excellent opportunities for growth in understanding and sustaining the Lutheran tradition.

Focusing on the distinctiveness of the college program, another variable is the key dimension of a school's *logos*. In recent years and out of the impulse of the Lutheran teachings on vocation, colleges have been paying increasing attention to Lutheran narratives in the construction of curricula. While "faith and learning" is not a Lutheran invention, it has always been central to the Lutheran intellectual tradition, and Lutherans have brought special resources to it. In the biblical, theological, and confessional narratives of the Lutheran tradition we find resources that apply to both the form and content of education. One thinks of Lutheran teachings on vocation, the two kingdoms, *simul justis et peccator*, original sin, and the priesthood of all believers. Or, with reference to the biblical tradition, one recognizes distinctive traditions of historical, literary, and rhetorical criticism. Concerning pedagogical matters, one thinks of the place of dialectic, the paradox, moral deliberation, and discernment in community.

The *pathos* of campus life is another significant variable in the unfolding of Lutheran identity and mission. Proclamation, prayer, and praise are staples of the Lutheran tradition and are formative of community. One calls to mind the worship centers on many campuses and the high-quality programs in sacred music and art that involve large numbers of students. Given the challenge posed by individualism in religious matters and the secularism of harried life styles, worship will be a challenge for this group of colleges. We will need creative and winsome leaders who can both gather students in and reach out to students where they gather. Given the impulse to serve others that is strongly present on our campuses, campus ministry will find ways to identify with and inform such endeavors. Under the aegis of Lilly-funded programs and churchwide initiatives, the vocation idea has taken root on many campuses and, increasingly, in the lives of many students. This trend is fortuitous for the mission and identity of these colleges.

I need to say that on most campuses the gathering of the community is increasingly problematic. Whether a lecture or a concert, a faculty meeting or morning coffee, a worship service or an athletic event, participation is a challenge. The busyness of the culture and the ubiquities of electronic communication combined with the individualism of the social order explain some of this. So in the coming decades we must continue to invent new modes of gathering the community and new strategies to build the unity and social coherence that is essential to the living out of our missions.

What of the variables related to the relationship of the colleges and the church? The new unit for Education and Vocation is intended to create synergies among the educational ministries of this church. Hopefully, the resources of theological education will enrich the colleges as they engage in the dialectic of faith and learning. On the other hand, the real world disciplines of the liberal arts colleges will be of benefit to the seminaries in their dialogue with a world of many faiths and cultures. There are some early and promising signs of collaboration; may their number multiply. The social statement on education prepared and adopted in 2007 calls upon bishops and pastors, churchwide and synods, to be more intentional in advocacy and support of the colleges. In turn, the colleges are called upon to affirm their unique identities as Lutheran colleges, to feature the Lutheran teaching on vocation, to maintain programs of liaison with various expressions of the church, and to collaborate in shared ministry projects. The embodiment of these commitments will go far in defining the relationship of college and church.

I have often described the current decade as a time of renaissance in mission for religious colleges in America. One sees signs of this revitalization at many turns. Many Lutheran colleges have been in the vanguard of this renaissance. Hopefully, this good beginning will provide the foundation for the continuing renewal of Lutheran colleges in coming decades. I believe in, and am committed to, such a future.

Works Cited

Richard Baepler, *The Church-Related College in an Age of Pluralism: The Quest for a Viable Saga* (Valparaiso, Indiana: Association of Lutheran College Faculty, 1977).

Robert Benne, *Quality with Soul: How Six Premier Colleges and Universities Keep Faith with Their Religious Traditions* (Grand Rapids, Michigan: Wm. B. Eerdmans Publishing Co., 2001).

James Tunstead Burtchaell, *The Dying of the Light: The Disengagement of Colleges and Universities from Their Christian Churches.* (Grand Rapids, Michigan: Wm. B. Eerdmans Publishing Co., 1998).

Harold H. Ditmanson, ed., *Christian Faith and the Liberal Arts* (Minneapolis: Augsburg Pubishing House, 1960).

Darrell Jodock, "The Lutheran Tradition and the Liberal Arts College: How Are They Related?" *Called to Serve: St. Olaf and the Vocation of a Church College*, Pamela Schwandt, Gary Stuart De Krey, and L. DeAne Lagerquist, eds. (Northfield, Minnesota: St. Olaf College, 1999), 13-36. (Found at http://gustavus.edu/faith/pdf/called_to_serve.pdf.)

George M. Marsden, *The Soul of the American University: From Protestant Establishment to Established Nonbelief* (New York: Oxford University Press, 1994).

Mark R. Schwehn, *Exiles from Eden: Religion and the Academic Vocation in America* (New York: Oxford University Press, 1993).

Douglas Sloan, *Faith and Knowledge: Mainline Protestantism and American Higher Education* (Louisville, Kentucky: Westminster John Knox, 1994).